Wood's Challenge (DWARF)

The endpaper shows L'Elégante, an ivy cultivar

Pelargoniums and Geraniums
A pocket guide

Henry J. Wood

John Bartholomew & Son Ltd
Edinburgh

Verona (GOLDEN LEAF)

© Henry J. Wood 1974.
First published in Great Britain 1974
by John Bartholomew and Son Ltd,
Duncan Street, Edinburgh EH9 1TA
and at 216 High Street, Bromley BR1 1PW

ISBN 085152 944 5

Printed in Great Britain

Contents

Hula (REGAL BACKCROSS)

The colour photographs are by
the author, Henry J. Wood

Acknowledgement

My thanks go to Mr. W. J. Webb, B.Sc., of Ealing, who has helped me by providing much information on the various species of *Geraniaceae*. A keen photographer, he has taken close-ups of the tiny flowers, and these interesting photographs, greatly enlarged, show all parts of the blooms in minute detail. Mr. Webb is also an expert artist in water-colours; this combination of talents surely makes him a leader among geranium specialists. He has himself written on the subject and has willingly shared his vast knowledge with me whenever I have needed it.

I record my great admiration for him in this book.

H. J. Wood

Ghost shoots on Freak of Nature

Foreword

Realising some twenty years ago the vast potential of the pelargonium, I decided to specialise in growing this plant, and to devote greater enthusiasm to it. Giving up the cultivation and showing of all the other species in which I had previously been interested really did pay dividends. Many people the world over have taken up this specialist interest.

In these chapters I have tried to bring before the reader just a small part of this most absorbing hobby. I have selected a few of the host of fascinating stories involving these plants, and have devoted some chapters to the differing characteristics of many of the myriad varieties—a number constantly increasing, by hybridisation, to meet the ever-growing demand, in contrast to the state of affairs two decades ago, when the plant was in the doldrums. My list of worthwhile varieties should guide the newcomer in his initial purchases, although thousands of excellent cultivars have been excluded due to lack of space.

Because of the current popularity of greenhouses, I have explained how to use them to best advantage.

This book has been written by an amateur for amateurs; the advice it contains may not apply to professionals, whose methods are geared to large-scale production. I hope that the pages which follow will encourage the reader to experiment with, cultivate, hybridise, and show *Geraniaceae*—a hobby of undoubted therapeutic value.

H. J. Wood.

Snowbank, Rhodamine, Buckhurst, Muriel Harris, Blythwood

Items of Interest

The outstanding feature of recent hybridisation is the emergence of large numbers of new regals and miniature zonals. There is brisk demand for new cultivars—hardly surprising when one considers how irresistible these beautiful plants look in their pots, and how reasonably priced most of them are.

Pelargoniums are ideal for impressive shows of colour outdoors because of their long flowering period; the brilliance of the zonal blooms can be reinforced by those of other plants, such as tagetes, alyssum, lobelia, coleus, and fuchsia. Doubtless the measure of hardiness now being bred into the regals will fit these for the same purpose; their use alongside zonals with coloured foliage will produce an incomparably dazzling show.

Pelargoniums are used in display not only in the British Isles but world-wide; in warm climates, they can be left outside all year; otherwise they must be taken indoors for the winter, and the grower can start anew with cuttings and regenerated plants. The very fact of beginning afresh each year keeps our interest alive—especially the business of taking cuttings—and provides considerable trade for nurseries. We are in this sense fortunate in having a partly deciduous plant which needs constant care and attention if perfection is sought, although it will stand a fair amount of neglect. The grower is thus provided with satisfying work and experimentation to do in his greenhouse.

There is widespread misunderstanding of the difference between pelargoniums and geraniums. The following few paragraphs may help to make the distinction clear.

All plants, whether cultivated or wild, are divided into "families" as a means of classification. The plants referred to in this book belong to the family *"Geraniaceae"*. This family is subdivided into what are termed "genera"; the geranium is one genus, the pelargonium another.

Present-day cultivated plants have been bred from types growing wild, referred to as "species". It is from the pelargonium, not from the geranium species, that our modern cultivated varieties are derived, a process begun well over two hundred years ago. So our Paul Crampels, Denmarks, Irenes, and types with coloured leaves, hybridised over many decades, are pelargoniums. Unfortunately, a few botanists in the past have created confusion by calling these cultivars "geraniums", the confusion being increased by the family name *Geraniaceae* (meaning geranium) and one of the genera called geranium. These two names should be entirely different.

Although geraniums proper have not been used for cross-pollination with present cultivated pelargoniums, they are very common in the wild state in the fields and hedgerows of Europe. Some worthwhile hardy examples of these, suitable for leaving out all year in the flowerbed or rockery, are mentioned elsewhere in this book.

The pelargonium-geranium mix-up is but one example of the confusion which exists in plant taxonomy (the classification of plants). The present system, although understood by the botanist, unfortunately leaves the ordinary gardener mystified; some intelligent simplification would put matters right, such as changing the family name.

In March, 1972, a geranium conservatory was opened in the botanic gardens at Geelong, Australia. The opening was attended by members of the local and other Victorian branches of the Australian Pelargonium and Geranium Society. The building, steel-framed with galvanised steel purlins supporting a fibreglass roof in the form of an octagonal pyramid, was constructed under the will of the late Miss F. E. Clark, who left twenty-two thousand dollars for this purpose. It is set against some lovely trees, including a Ginkgo Biloba tree planted soon after the opening of the gardens in about 1830.

The cultivation of the pelargonium can easily become an all-consuming passion. If you find this happening, you will no doubt want to read around the subject as there is much of

Madame Everaarts (DWARF)

relevance to be learned in such studies as botany, hydroponics, and taxonomy. I have found all the old biological and gardening books I can buy at a reasonable price of great value in helping me to understand the subject, as well as being a pleasure to read. Such works as Darwin's "Origin of Species" and "Forms of Flowers", Mendel's "Principles of Heredity", and a host of others from the nineteenth century offer something not to be found in more modern ones, and the vocabulary is so very different. These old gems are worth seeking out since the more scientific this age becomes, the more one needs to go back into the past to try to recover something of the peace of mind of by-gone days.

Characteristics of Certain Types

P. frutetorum

The King of the Boars

This most interesting plant has appeared in recent years. It was hybridised by Miss Mary Campbell, who used The Boar as one parent. This fast-growing plant should, with good cultivation, soon be ready to exhibit. To avoid confusion, it should not be grown along with The Boar. The latter is inclined to the prostrate habit, but usually reverts to the upright after a time.

The prostrate hybrid is more vigorous than the original, and is useful in hanging baskets, where it will produce abundant single orange flowers in summer. If so used, it should be cut back or stopped early on in its growth; this prevents the laterals from becoming too long and encourages many new breaks which are of great advantage in smothering the circumference of the basket with foliage. The cuttings are useful for propagation. The very dark centre of the leaf makes the plant attractive for use in floral displays when used in conjunction with zonal flowers.

The cultivar has excellent qualities for the purposes of breeding, and could profitably be crossed with all other types. The seedlings should inherit its extreme vigour. My suggested cross is with the Deacons.

At the time of writing, I have seen the outcome of some of Miss Campbell's predictions. She has succeeded in adding some fairly large flowers to this remarkable power of growth and, instead of single blooms standing above the foliage, the new hybrids have umbels of far greater substance.

The deep markings on the leaves of this species are evidence of a dominant black pigment which has greatly influenced the hybrids of many hortorums. *P. zonal*, although it has achieved distinction as one of the main parents of the hortorums, does not have this feature to the same extent. *P. frutetorium* has great potential as a parent due not only to its dark pigmentation but also to the vigour shown by many of the cultivars of this group. The word "group" in this context is not universally accepted at the time of writing, but it probably will become so because of the increasing number of hybrids originating from it all over the world, many still unnamed and unclassified. Those recorded so far are:

DARK BEAUTY. Dark green leaves with black central blotches. Single orange flowers. Prostrate habit.

MAGIC LANTERN. Zoned leaf, light green with reds and yellows.

MEDALLION. Golden leaves with brown and red central blotches.

MOSAIC. Dark foliage with light green markings. Single pink flowers.

PROSTRATE BOAR. Small, heavily zoned leaves. Pink flowers.

ROYAL. Dark green leaves with even darker centres.

THE BOAR. Upright habit, sometimes tending to prostrate. Single pink flowers.

FLORAL CASCADE. Possibly one of the greatest plants of the century, it has semi-double, wide-open, rich pink flowers. In common with the Prostrate Boar, one of its parents, it has the trailing habit of the ivies but is far more robust. In time, both of these hybrids should replace the ivies.

ENDLESS JOY. A seedling from Floral Cascade. Single deep pink flowers, with thirty two-inch pips per head. Vigorous growth. No deep zone in leaf.

GAZELLE. Dark foliage. Pink flowers. Hybridised by Miss Campbell. Similar to Magic Lantern.

The members of the above group, into which large flowers have now been introduced, make good growth and are easy to propagate. Used together with other types, they are extremely useful in hanging baskets. Breeders in Australia, America, and England have great expectations of these hybrids, which will probably replace the ivy-leaved types to some extent.

Miniature Ivy

GAY BABY. (Not to be confused with Pink Gay Baby.) This miniature ivy-leaved cultivar from Australia has caused some interest. Although small it is extremely vigorous and will give plenty of easily rooted cuttings in a short time. Its origin is unknown, but its appearance suggests *P. saxifragoides* as one parent. Growth is always compact: in rapid succession leaves are formed which overlap each other in perfect formation, due to very short internodes. As this trait is so predominant, the plant would be ideal for breeding purposes. The flowers, although small and well suited to the growth habit, could be improved, and other colours introduced.

Gay Baby is ideally suited to cultivation in a polypropylene "bloom bottle". This has a reservoir underneath which, by means of a wick, keeps the compost damp by capillary action.

Veined Ivy Leaves

WHITE MESH (or Sussex Lace). A sport from Madame Crousse. Deep green leaf, coarsely grained. Semi-double flower.
CROCODILE. Finely veined leaves. Small, single, red flower.

The ivy-shaped leaves of White Mesh and Crocodile show lovely veining which has caused some controversy. It is said to be due to a non-spreading, harmless, vein-clearing virus. The symptoms are similar to those of "yellow net vein" virus, deemed in the States to be harmful to plants; there, plants showing signs of this are to be destroyed. In England, there is no evidence that these two cultivars, which were discovered in Australia, are unhealthy: millions of cuttings are successfully propagated every year.

Blythwood, Aztec (REGALS)

Crocodile was named by the late Ted Both of Adelaide, who came across it in his nursery. One batch, it is said, was to be shipped from America to England, but a mistake was made: White Mesh was sent instead. The importer disliked the name "Crocodile" and renamed the variety "Sussex Lace". This has led to a great deal of confusion. To quote Miss Carpenter, writing in the journal of the Australian Pelargonium and Geranium Society in Victoria,

"in the name of British fair play, to say nothing of plain common sense, why cannot this irritating and misleading Sussex Lace misnomer be discontinued?"

It is worth considering whether the non-spreading virus could be introduced into ordinary green zonal leaves; this could be an added attraction.

Both's Stellars

These were originally called Both's Staphs; this was entirely misleading. It was assumed that his plants had originated from *P. staphysagroides,* as the leaves of his hybrids resembled those of this species. There is now some doubt as to whether *P. staphysagroides* is an original species. It is fairly certain that Both's Stellars had, as one parent, the Chinese Cactus; this has a deeply indented dark-zoned leaf, a feature inherited by the hybrids. There is no doubt that various zonals were used also.

The appropriate name Stellar was chosen by Mr. Bagust of Wyck Hill Geraniums, the first nursery to import the plants into England; this was in 1966, the exporter being Mr. W. H. Wood of Highett, Victoria. The transaction was made possible by the influence of the late Mr. W. H. Heytman, also of Victoria, a well-known personality in Australian pelargonium circles. Wyck Hill Geraniums now list twelve Stellars.

Ted Both bred hundreds of these plants, many of which were sub-standard and were therefore wisely discarded. He died with his work unfinished. Very few specimens were named; the rest, which bore numbered tags, were given names by Messrs. John R. Blackman and Robert F. G. Swinbourne.

These hybrids could be further developed. The unique pattern of their leaves gives them wide sales appeal and they are easy to grow and propagate. There are both single and double varieties of flower. The lower petals are broad and wedge-shaped, with a serrated edge; the upper ones are sharply forked and much narrower.

The Deacon Cultivars

These were based on the ivy-leaved Blue Peter and the miniature Orion, and have proved themselves to be an excellent cross. They were bred by the Rev. Stanley Stringer of Occold, Suffolk, England, the originator of some first-class miniatures. The Deacons represent a departure from his usual hybrids. They are worthwhile because they are short-jointed with compact, bushy growth and ample bloom to match. The Rev. Stringer emphasises that their main features are their free flowering habit and long season in bloom, even at low temperatures. The Deacon pelargoniums, which may well dominate the shows in the years ahead, were introduced at Chelsea in 1970 by Wyck Hill Geraniums, Stow-on-the-Wold, Glos., England.

The True Geranium

For ground cover, or in the rockery, try *sanguineum album*, pure white flowers; *subcaulescenes*, red, dark-centred flowers; *pylzowianum*, pink flowers; *stapfianum roseum*, crimson flowers; *dalmaticum*, clear pink flowers, leaves turning russet in autumn; *dalmaticum* can also have white flowers; *sessiliflorum*, with white flowers, has one interesting variety with lovely lobed leaves of grey-green sponge-like appearance; *renardii* grows to a height of about ten inches; *nodosum* has glossy, clear-cut leaves and small lilac flowers on stems twelve inches tall. All of the above hardy plants are easily grown in any soil.

Several years ago, an American grower sent me a few seeds. The emergent plants were potted and promptly inserted in open ground in the garden. Due to lack of space in the greenhouses, I had to leave many plants outside in the winter, knowing they would probably perish. Among them were the true geranium *maculatum* and an erodium, *hymonedes*. Both plants survived, in spite of six inches of snow and ice. Although *maculatum* did suffer some leaf spoilage, it soon showed its hardiness, no doubt due to its North American origin, by putting on fresh leaves at an early date.

G. maculatum's main attraction is its foliage. Pale green leaves emerge from the base of the plant. Tiny red stems then grow to a length of about twelve inches, turning crimson in the process. The finely cut leaves turn a darker green with age, and in the autumn show the colours typical of that season, due to the dominant tendency to redness in the plant. The leaves will retain their form for some time if placed between sheets of clear polythene; their colour can be preserved by pressing between layers of paper.

G. maculatum can be used to advantage in large display boxes or tubs, but its ungainly flowering stems, which can reach two feet in length, must be kept under control or they will detract from the beauty of the leaves. The plant produces a fair number of self-sown seedlings.

I quote the following from the Morden Geranium Nursery's catalogue: "Hardy Geraniums. The true geranium species. Hardy herbaceous and alpine plants flowering for a long period, useful for the border, rock garden, or wild garden. The larger kinds will give a second display if cut to the ground when flowering is nearly finished."

The proprietor of the nursery, Mr. Sid White, is keenly interested in the geranium genus; his latest list contains twenty varieties, all of which are recommended. They display great variety in size and in the shape of their leaves, and seed well.

Formosum

An excitingly novel pelargonium from Merry Gardens, Camden, Maine, U.S.A. It has dense clusters of white-tipped salmon flowers on stout stems and small leaves, irregularly lobed, and will bloom abundantly throughout the year. *Variegated Fragrans*. A specimen of this lovely miniature was once given to me as a gift. I left it on a high shelf for the winter. With the coming of spring, my attention was drawn to the plant and several cuttings were taken with ease.

I had difficulty in tracing its origin since it was not listed by nurserymen at that time, though it is now, and text-books were of little help. The nearest approach was a reference in a book by Derek Clifford to a variegated form of *P. odoratissimum*. This species has apple-scented leaves whereas Variegated Fragrans has the scent of the original Fragrans. This seems to contradict the theory that *P. odoratissimum* is the parent of *P. fragrans*.

Variegated Fragrans makes a delightful gift. Quite apart from its marvellous perfume, its form and habit are ideal for a miniature, with short internodes. It is always compact, a plant six inches tall and equally wide having about one hundred tiny leaves from one-quarter to one inch in size. The well-cut leaves are pale green inside and lemon yellow outside, but no two are identical. Its tiny flowers suit the structure of the plant very well.

Lavender Grand Slam (REGAL)

Display and Showing

The simplest ways of displaying these plants are to grow them in pots, standing on saucers for window decoration, and to use them in wire baskets hanging in the porch. Pelargoniums will keep well inside the windows in both summer and winter, provided there is adequate light; a south-facing aspect produces the healthiest, most luxuriant specimens. Plants should be turned regularly to ensure uniform growth.

Many arrangements can be made with from ten to twenty pots on the sill, but these look better with plastic covers. Alternatively, the plants can be accommodated in a trough on the inside sill or in a window-box outside. Choose paintwork to match the rest of the décor. The presence of the living plants makes a remarkable difference to the home, producing a cheerful atmosphere in place of the rather clinical one prevailing in so many modern houses. The use of large picture windows, a modern trend, is an inducement to produce fine floral displays such as are seen in almost every window on the Continent—particularly in Belgium—where, however, the frequent poor variety of colour could easily be improved by the use of a few pelargoniums. You have a choice between plants that need constant renewal and more lasting ones which can be moved to new positions occasionally to prevent monotony. Varieties such as Dolly Varden and Aberanth, which have beautifully coloured leaves and which flourish indoors, are recommended since, even in the absence of flowers, the foliage adds such charm to a window display, especially when viewed from outside.

Polypropylene pots are the best for home or greenhouse use. They can easily be washed with mild disinfectant fluid; mould and fungus do not adhere to them; they are warm to the touch, so that the task of washing them in winter is made more pleasant; and they can be written on with crayon. This is a useful method of labelling the plants since the name, although easily removed with a rag, will not fade in the normal course of events. Incidentally, those readers with an artistic bent can use the crayons to draw their favourite plants or to make tracings of their leaves.

A plant taken to a flower show will often resent the journey and show its disapproval on arriving home, however carefully it is handled. This is due to the changes in watering, heating, lighting, and air that it has to put up with for three days. A

Muriel Hawkins (REGAL)

similar environmental shock occurs when a plant is sent through the post or by rail no matter how well it is packed.

When exhibiting plants, keep insects away from them. They tend to pollinate the flowers with the result that the petals drop off the pips, nature's way of clearing dead matter from the seeds so that rot does not form on them. This trouble is more prevalent with doubles than with singles.

Photography

Pelargoniums make ideal subjects for colour photography. The flowers of the regal group make some of the most glamorous studies; here the close-up lens comes into its own. Care must be taken when focusing the camera on the bloom since parallax error at distances of less than six feet can lead to trouble. Whether you use the reflex type or some other, consult the "camera-to-subject" advice given in your instruction booklet.

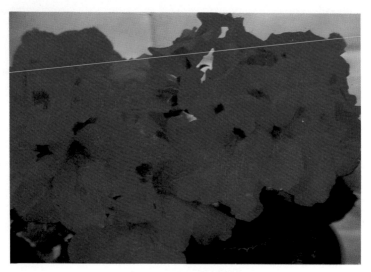

Grand Slam (REGAL)

In taking shots of cultivars with coloured leaves, concentrate on the foliage. Do fit some part of the flower in, though, to help you to recognise the variety later, since the foliage differs less from one type to another than the blooms do.

A 35 mm camera capable of producing transparencies is far cheaper to run than one which makes colour prints, and reproduces the original shades more faithfully, although it does necessitate the purchase of a projector and a screen. Different makes of film produce surprisingly different colours; experiment will tell you which gives the best results.

Photographic slides are essential if you wish to lecture at horticultural society meetings. They are useful, too, for exchanging with fellow enthusiasts overseas; if you do this, be sure to take several shots of any specially selected subject.

One of the earliest ideas I implemented on becoming P.R.O. of the then Geranium Society was to take coloured slides of the hundreds of different types of flowers and plants that were available to me. The intention was to lend these transparencies to universities, horticultural societies, and clubs, on free loan. Editors in the gardening press kindly obliged me with notices in their papers, publicising the service. Although all of this was hard on my pocket, it had the desired results to such an extent that, after about five years, the job of lending the slides got beyond me, and I had to stop. In all, I have taken about two thousand photographs of the *Geraniaceae* family; some of them have been used to illustrate this book.

Horticultural societies, local and national, would do well to encourage more of their members to make transparencies for projection at meetings; it stimulates interest and friendly rivalry.

Cultivation

Treatment of New Plants

New plants from a nursery or shop must be very carefully treated as it is at this stage that most loss occurs due to ignorance and bad handling. Protect them in a frame for the first two weeks to harden them off, even if this has already been done by the propagator. In the absence of a proper frame, use four boards of a width suited to the height of the plants, and cover the top with glass or clear plastic. Even an old box, with or without the bottom knocked out, will give some protection until the new arrivals get acclimatised. They should not be coddled; give them as much air as possible short of a cold draught. Do not place soft plants directly into the ground, even in early summer, as this will lead to defoliation. These precautions prevent poor quality in the later stages of growth and give greater resistance to disease.

It is disastrous to water the leaves with cold tap-water at this early stage. Always use water with the chill taken off; pure rainwater collected, for example, in a barrel from the greenhouse roof, is best at this and all other times.

Do not feed the plants until they have become established. Although excessive watering will cause rot, the roots should be kept reasonably moist.

Soil Management

The most important prerequisite to healthy plants, resistant to disease and insect attack, is good soil. Conditioning the ground should be started in the first year and continued every year thereafter. It is best to follow the "law of return": put back into the earth all that has been taken from it and more. No garden should be without a compost heap. Throw everything from grass clippings to kitchen vegetable waste on to it, avoiding weed seeds, and add layers of ammonium sulphate to encourage the bacteria to do their beneficial work. Even fish bones and skin help. Cinders and ash from burning paper and wood can be added to the soil. They contain carbon, the element most essential to life.

Dig the ground one spit deep and bury such things as rotting clothes made from natural fibres. Digging in an old flock mattress evenly will yield some of the finest specimens you have ever seen. Do not, however, make a hard pan, such as a pad of paper, directly under the plants: this would restrict root growth. Be sure all matter is mixed well with the soil.

To improve sandy soil, lay clods of clay, obtainable from building sites, on top of it early in the winter, and let the weather break them down. Humus, in the form of leaves and peat, is also of some value here, although it quickly decomposes and is absorbed by plants hungry for the nourishment generally lacking in sandy soil. Digging in cinders or ash will help the ground to retain moisture.

Conversely, clay soil benefits from the addition of sand as

Madame Butterfly (DWARF), see centre leaf

well as humus and cinders.

Success in building up the soil may be gauged fairly well by the level of the surrounding beds and pathways. The presence of worms in the earth is another good sign; if there are none there, much more humus is required. The addition of humus should always take place well before planting to allow soil bacteria to break it down into an easily assimilated form.

The importance of charcoal cannot be overstressed. It sweetens and, when it disintegrates, builds up the soil or soilless compost, as the case may be. In days of yore, gardeners used old soot and manure water to produce good results. The following extract is from "Loudon's Plain Instruction in Gardening", published in 1874, and written by Jane, the wife of the great botanist J. C. Loudon:

"No plant has been more improved than the Pelargonium by the new system of rough potting, and mixing the soil with charcoal. According to the old plan, the loamy soil in which the Geraniums were planted soon caked together, and became so hard as to be alike impervious to water and air. I have myself found the ball of earth of a geranium hard and dry in the centre, though I had watered it every day. When this is the case, the plants, being deprived of their proper supply of carbon, become weak and etiolated, and are more disposed to produce stems and leaves than flowers.

By the system of rough potting, on the contrary, air and water are admitted freely to the roots; and the consequence is that the plants are compact in shape, and covered with superb flowers."

Soot, in these days of smokeless zones, is a very scarce commodity but charcoal can be bought, although it is rather expensive, or produced by burning old timber. Plants receive most of their carbon from carbon dioxide present in the air, by the process known as "photosynthesis".

A liberal dressing of bone meal or iron sulphate is beneficial to the soil if it does not already contain enough iron. This element is an important one in growing tough, healthy plants. Lime is another essential: a good quantity should be applied just before planting. Lime breaks down many components of the soil and should not, therefore, be used at the same time as other fertilisers. If it is distributed too early, many of the ingredients you added will be leached out by the rain: the soil structure will no longer be able to hold them. This effect is not generally realised. Lime is also a cleansing agent. Many gardeners regard it as purely a fertiliser and wrongly assume that the addition of further organic or inorganic material is unnecessary.

Soilless Composts

These many and varied mixes are now widely used and have

My compost mixture for potting

largely superseded soil-based composts which, with their quota of diseases and pests, needed costly sterilisation. Heat was used for this with the destruction of the good bacteria along with the bad, much to the detriment of the plants. Soilless composts, on the other hand, are usually completely sterile to begin with. Nutrients can easily be added in the form of liquid fertiliser. The use of these composts, in preference to those containing soil, is strongly advised.

The new mixtures are based on peat, either sphagnum or sedge, coarse or sharp sand, and vermiculite of various grades used separately or in any combination. I prefer to mix my own. I then know exactly how to apply different fertilisers to suit the individual requirements of the various pelargoniums I grow. The plants, be they cuttings, young specimens or more mature ones, are potted in my standard mixture and their feed is frequently varied according to the appearance of the foliage. The knowledge of how to do this comes with experience.

My mix of coarse sand, peat, and vermiculite has a very open structure, so frequent watering is needed in hot weather, which is an advantage to an amateur as a weak feed can be given with each watering. This is much better than a strong dose infrequently applied. Professional growers cannot work this way because of the extra labour involved; their problem can be solved by the use of plastic pots which, not being porous, help to retain moisture. These pots are preferable to clay ones but are often blamed for failures really caused by over-compactness of the soil. Another advantage of an open compost is that air can penetrate to all parts of the root fibres, allowing the fine, hair-like roots to grow without hindrance.

The use of a ready-made compost, such as John Innes, saves trouble. Be sure, though, that you go to a supplier with a quick turnover of stock: the mixture deteriorates in storage and could become so stale as to kill your plants.

Feeding and Watering

Pelargoniums flourish after a rainy period, evidence that they do need water. A feed of potash at this time helps to toughen up their tissues and gives extra colour to the flowers. Nitrogen should not be applied in wet weather.

To quote again from Mrs. Loudon's book, "Pelargoniums require a great deal of air and when about to flower they should have a great deal of water, but at other seasons very little. They are killed with the slightest frost and they are liable to damp off, if watered too much, and not allowed sufficient air, in winter. Air is, indeed, quite essential to them."

The feeding a plant needs depends on its environment and on the weather. No hard and fast rules can be given, but "little and often" is a good motto during the growing season, especially in dry weather when a small drop of liquid nutrient can be

Cuttings rooted in "Phostrogen" fluid

put into the watering-can each time it is filled. As the season progresses, the plants should build up into sturdy specimens and, towards the end, feeding can be discontinued.

Unlike animals, plants can assimilate nourishment in liquid form only. Solids need to be broken down and dissolved in water before they can enter the plants' tissues.

Research in government and private laboratories and experimental stations has led to detailed knowledge of liquid fertilisers and how to use them to optimum advantage. The product "Phostrogen" is an excellent liquid feed for pelargoniums and will supply all your plants' needs whatever compost you employ. It can be used both for rooting cuttings and for growing on, and is especially recommended for the ivy-leaved varieties and for hanging baskets. Until you gain suffi-

33

Brighton Belle. Bred by Mary Campbell

**Seedling Lemon Fancy. Mabel Gray × Prince of Orange
Bred by Helen Bowie.**

cient experience to judge the correct dose in individual cases, follow the instructions on the bottle.

When a plant has become mature, change from Phostrogen to a tomato fertiliser, or add potash and magnesium.

Liquid fertilisers are very cheap considering the returns they give. Poor plants indicate a stingy gardener, unwilling to spend time and money. It has very little to do with "green fingers". Well-fed, healthy plants are less susceptible to attack by disease and aphids, can stand up better to fungicides and insecticides, and recover more quickly if some ailment does strike.

Bindweed (or "Bellbine")

This weed is noted for its binding power both above and below ground. The menace can be eradicated by planting up the infested ground with pelargoniums. The parts of the weed above ground tend to be torn away but this stimulates new growth on the roots. Bindweed roots cannot live alongside those of pelargoniums, and rapidly succumb.

Pelargoniums for Christmas Decoration

Experiment has shown me that, contrary to popular belief, cuttings, even when struck late, can be brought into bloom during November and December. Probably it is lack of demand that has discouraged nurserymen from putting pelargoniums on the Christmas market, but a bit of publicity could alter this. After Christmas, the plants can be grown on until they are fairly large, and placed in the garden in spring. The same cannot be said of many of the other plants specially coddled for sale in the festive season.

Fluorescent lighting applied for two hours after sunset each evening and electrical heating of the compost are essential for quick rooting. Once the cuttings have rooted, they must be potted immediately and kept under the lights.

Fasciation

There are many cultivars that will bloom at Christmas. Large flowers are not of first importance in this case. After the first flush of bloom is over, further buds should be removed in order to prepare the plants for outdoor use.

Fasciation

This phenomenon occurs mainly with zonal pelargoniums in spring. It consists of the appearance of one or more smaller flowers above the normal flower head, and can be induced by increased watering or feeding after the winter resting period. It usually clears itself up in a few weeks and does not seem to harm the plants.

Greenhouse Management

Be sure to purchase the largest greenhouse that your pocket and garden area permit. It is more economical to do this than to buy a second one when you find that your growing interest has rendered the first one too small. Also, it is cheaper to heat one large house than two small ones. The type made of cedar is recommended. The glass should extend nearly down to ground level so that the space under the staging receives enough light to make it useful; this will increase the storage capacity of the greenhouse by about a quarter.

Sliding and outward-opening doors are preferable to inward-opening ones, which are inconvenient in many ways. There should be at least one vent on each side of the top of the house and one in the back wall to ensure adequate ventilation.

A propagating frame on one of the benches will ensure quick, successful rooting of cuttings. Electricity can be used to heat the rooting compost, the current flowing in wires or heating tapes; this accelerates rooting and helps to prevent the stagnation which tends to occur in unheated soil, which can turn cold and sour. Heated soil does require the frequent application of fresh moisture, but this is in any case what most living plants require.

Select your ideal rooting compost by trial and error. Sand, vermiculite and peat can be used separately or in any combination. If using peat, put in some form of lime to counteract its acidity. If all three are used together, add some granulated charcoal to keep the mixture sweet.

A frame can easily be made from half-inch timber, six inches wide; three feet by five is a convenient size. If the staging is slatted, cover it with wire mesh and on top of that

Plants growing in black polypots

place a layer of polythene to help retain moisture. The polythene should be perforated to allow surplus water to drain
away. A sixty-watt fluorescent tube about eighteen inches above
the frame is a very useful aid to growth. About sixteen feet of
tape or wire buried three inches deep should suffice to heat
the compost. When all the rooted cuttings have been removed
the frame can be either left *in situ* and used to accommodate
pot plants, or dismantled and removed, to be reassembled
later in the year.

Cultivation in a greenhouse is quite different from that
outdoors due to the protection afforded by the structure.
Plants should be given as much fresh air as possible, especially
if paraffin heating is employed.

Mature pot plants left outside all summer to supplement

ground plantings can be taken inside the greenhouse and stored under the staging, provided that the glass extends nearly down to ground level, although plants stored in this way require more attention than those on the benches: a good circulation of air must be maintained and dead leaves removed frequently, which will aid the flow of air. Dust well with a fungicide such as Captan, Zineb or Bordeaux powder at the beginning of storage and discourage a damp atmosphere. It may be helpful to prune the plants down a bit, but don't forget to dust the cuts with Captan. The prunings can be rooted in pots or in the frame.

Cuttings taken late in the season should be left undisturbed in the rooting frame or pots in spite of their becoming rather leggy: potting up in winter can lead to heavy losses. In any case the tops of leggy plants make useful propagating material early in the new year. Never be afraid to stop or cut back your plants in early spring; it is often very beneficial, although it should not be done if you wish to exhibit them.

In winter a temperature of about 42 degrees Farenheit is suitable for most pelargoniums. If this is exceeded, the plants will grow soft and will not harden off quickly. The optimum temperature depends on whether they are to be put out into the garden for the summer or kept in the greenhouse all year, a practice suited, for example, to the delightful, easily-propagated miniature range.

Paraffin is the most economical source of heat. For maximum efficiency, equipment should be kept clean; wicks should be trimmed daily during the running period. Modern lamps do very little damage, if any, to foliage provided ventilation is adequate at all times. Golden foliage is the type most vulnerable to fumes and will show some spoilage. To obtain good heat distribution without fumes, place the lamp several feet away from one side or end of the house and fix a horizontal tube from the top of the lamp leading outside, to dispose of the unwanted gases. This tube will act as an effective retainer of heat, whereas a vertical one would not.

Cutting back a "leggy" plant.

Ready for leaf axils

Paraffin, although economical, requires manual control of its heat output. Electricity, however, is useful where the greenhouse owner cannot be on hand all the time, as the temperature can be controlled by means of a rod thermostat. Also, this device partly offsets the higher cost of electricity by cutting out excess production of heat. In areas liable to power cuts, a paraffin heater should be kept as a stand-by.

A polythene lining inside the greenhouse will reduce costs by conserving heat, and will act as a second line of defence in the event of a pane of glass breaking, protecting the plants against wind and frost until a repair can be effected. It has, however, the unfortunate tendency to increase humidity to the point of dampness, particularly if the heater is of a type that gives off water vapour. Humidity is desirable for most of the year, as it prevents the drying out of plants and cuttings, but it must be avoided in winter by adequate ventilation, short of actually chilling the plants; any drips running from the polythene on to the plants could be fatal. The lining should be so arranged that this possibility is reduced.

The plastic on the inside of the roof should be left in position during the summer, unless the weather is persistently wet and dull. It will protect the contents of the house from the direct rays of the sun, obviating the need for blinds or shading paint. Lining the entire interior of the greenhouse would encourage dampness, especially in winter, so it is best to leave the lower half of the glass uncovered, the area at your discretion.

Polythene sheeting is within the reach of everyone's pocket. It is sold in three thicknesses, all of which are suitable. The heavier grade lasts longer but reduces light penetration and becomes dirty if left up too long, whereas the thinner material can be replaced more frequently due to its low cost, and allows more light to enter. The 200-gauge sheeting is quite efficient, but experiment is necessary to find which grade suits particular conditions best.

During the winter, polythene should not be used to cover the slats on benches, since the circulation of air around the pots must not be obstructed, and trays containing gravel should not be used. These precautions reduce dampness. A fan heater properly used aids ventilation without causing undue draughts.

Ordinary newspaper is ideal for conserving heat during very cold weather. Layers of it can be laid on top of the plants when necessary and removed when the atmosphere warms up next morning; the foliage then has a fresh appearance. The paper, which must be kept dry, can, if the need arises, be left on the plants for several days, in which case the leaves will suffer no more than a slight loss of their lovely green colour.

Watering in the greenhouse should be done with pure water, such as fresh rain-water collected in a tank or tub. Such a container should be drained regularly and washed with a solution of Jeyes Fluid. Unclean water, stagnant from lying around for weeks, perhaps in a contaminated container, can cause damping off disease. This spreads quickly, particularly in damp conditions. If plants really need water during the winter, it must be kept off the foliage and staging.

Tap-water can be very harmful to certain plants, especially when hot weather dries out the compost very quickly, causing a concentration in the pots of chemicals added to the water during purification. This danger is less likely outside in the garden since the water is spread over a wider area; also, rain will wash the unwanted chemicals away.

Spring is the season when most watchfulness and attention are required to ensure first-class specimens. It is then that a plant takes on new life and begins to grow vigorously; satisfactory succulence in both stems and leaves, so much sought after by good growers, will be assured if, at this time, the moisture content in the compost is always kept sufficiently high.

A reliable thermometer is most useful in the greenhouse to give a quick indication of changing weather conditions, and to warn when heating is required. The simple single-bulb type will do, but the more expensive maximum-minimum instrument is the best; it shows what the highest and lowest temperatures have been since it was last set.

The greenhouse will provide you with work all the year round, as there is generally something to be attended to even in winter. Make up your mind which plant family you intend to grow in it and exclude all others, since the conditions of heat etc. which suit one family ideally will not be the best for another. The pelargonium family embraces so many cultivars and species that discretion is necessary, even within this group, in choosing which type to cultivate and which to leave alone. There is much to be said for specialisation in one genus.

Propagation

Professionals with heated propagating equipment can take cuttings all year round. The amateur should do so from February to October only as November, December, and January are very poor months for the supply of cuttings; if they are available then, bottom heat must be applied from cables in the rooting medium, and overhead fluorescent tubes should be

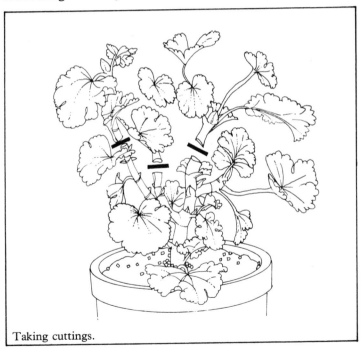

Taking cuttings.

used to shorten the rooting period and give good, clean plants. The additional light aids photosynthesis. As few leaves as possible should be removed since they are responsible for the production of roots in the cutting.

Fluorescent tubes, being fairly cool while running, will not scorch the plants, but cannot be relied on as a supplementary heat source. Tungsten bulbs operate at much higher temperatures and so are useful in maintaining a dry atmosphere, but they must not be placed too close to the foliage.

Cuttings should be taken three or four inches long (although slips one inch long can be used quite easily). They should have a well-balanced appearance, especially if you intend to sell them, but do not worry too much about this as unshapeliness at this stage can soon be straightened out to produce a good final result.

Using a razor blade, make your cut on the stem just above a node, i.e., a leaf-joint. Dust the surface of the incision on the mother plant. The cutting should now have its lower internode removed so that it terminates just below a leaf-joint. A callus will appear on the cut surface and roots will develop behind it. Any small length of stem left below the joint might set up rot which may travel upwards.

Cleanliness is of paramount importance in preventing the spread of infection: immerse the blade frequently in a fungicidal solution, and dip the lower end of the cutting in a fungicidal rooting powder to prevent disease spores from entering the wound. Powder which does not contain fungicide should be avoided since one infected cutting dipped into it will contaminate it with disease which is then transmitted to others.

A little coarse sand inserted at the base of the cutting, where it contacts the soil or compost, encourages quicker rooting.

Do not let the cutting dry out before placing it in the compost. Professional propagators spray with water in the form of a mist to keep the leaves fresh, especially with subjects that do not root easily.

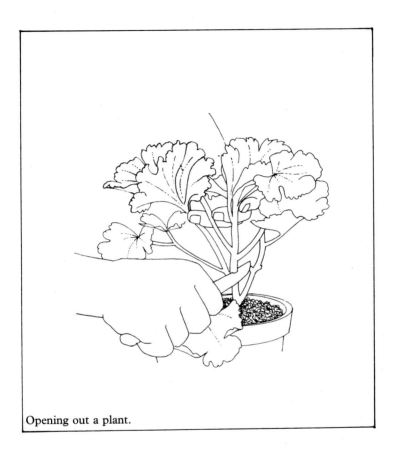

Opening out a plant.

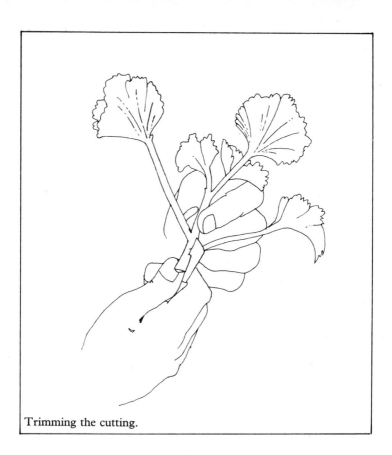

Trimming the cutting.

Leaf axils

Leaf-axil cuttings are becoming widely used. Look for a tiny bud growing at the base of a leaf, where it joins the main stem. Cut right through the stem about one-quarter of an inch above and below the selected axil, still retaining the leaf, and, using a sharp blade, make a cut down the piece of stem you have removed. Discard the offside piece, dip the leaf-axil in rooting powder, knock off any surplus, and immediately insert the cutting into compost. This method is more successful during the growing season than at other times. It can be very useful in building up stock.

When your cuttings begin to put on a lot of top growth, stop them to enable them to become strong, bushy, healthy specimens. "Stopping" means pinching out the tip of the plant and causes it to produce "breaks" or "shoots" from below the stopping point. The lower the break, the better the future plant. When you gain experience, you will not be afraid to cut back drastically, although a reasonable number of nodes must be retained for the further production of fresh growths.

Stopping radically alters the character and structure of the plants. The stems thicken and broaden out making for the bushiness that is so much sought after. The roots grow faster, encouraging better top growth.

In nearly all plant life, the main energy of a seedling or cutting goes into producing blooms and seeds for repro-duction. It follows that if you remove the initial flowers and buds, this energy is diverted into increasing growth both above and below ground, although the determination to flower is still there, and a better plant results. Chrysanthemums intended for exhibitions, where large flowers and leaves are required, are always stopped and then disbudded.

Cuttings received by post should be soaked in water or, better, in a hydroponic solution of Phostrogen for about twelve hours. Such treatment replaces moisture lost in transit and provides nourishment to ensure healthy root growth.

Propagation of zonal pelargoniums from seed is a frustrating business unless you use the "Carefree" strain. Many growers are finding these seeds successful although the cost is rather high compared with that of taking cuttings from named varieties. Many pelargoniums, geraniums, and erodiums can, however, be economically grown from seed. This is an easy way of building up a good stock if you have a large garden. All true geraniums and some erodiums are hardy perennials, with beautiful foliage; many are only six inches tall and are therefore suitable for the rockery. The erodium *macradenum*, with violet veined flowers, and the geranium *candidum*, which has white flowers with purple centres, are both miniatures.

Seeds from the pelargonium and geranium species usually give good results and run true to type, but are not as readily available as growing plants. In England, Thompson and Morgan of Ipswich offer seeds for five types of erodium, twenty of geranium and five of pelargonium. There are a few other well-established firms of pelargonium specialists in both England and America who supply seeds from their own selected stocks of miniatures. If you cannot find what you want in the catalogues of these reputable suppliers, do not buy the so-called geranium seeds sold in packets, as these yield plants with plenty of foliage but practically no blooms. Those flowers which do materialise usually take about eighteen months to mature. It is better to take seeds from your own stock. Also, these can be exchanged with other enthusiasts, but the greatest pleasure lies in cross-breeding.

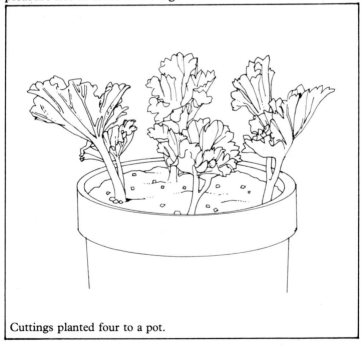

Cuttings planted four to a pot.

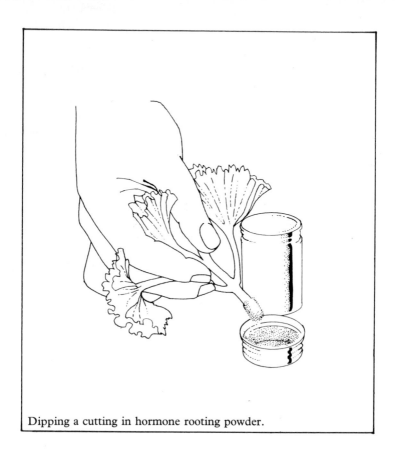

Dipping a cutting in hormone rooting powder.

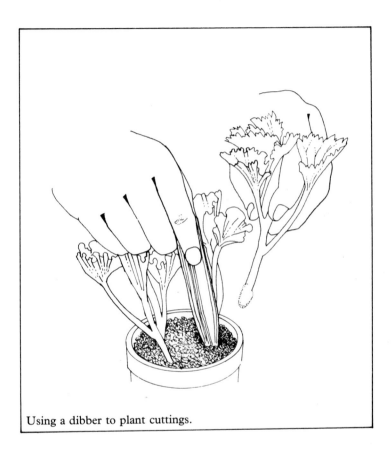

Using a dibber to plant cuttings.

Hybridisation

The Englishman Peter Grieve was a leading breeder of cultivars with coloured leaves. A hundred years ago, he wrote a very authoritative book entitled "A History of Ornamental Foliaged Pelargoniums". On page twenty-three of that work, he suggested that breeders should try to get rid of the unsightly crumpling of leaves, caused by the green centres' outgrowing the silver edges, giving a concave effect. A typical example of this is in Flower of Spring.

A few years ago, I received a cutting tagged Improved Flower of Spring. From this, many thousands of plants have been propagated. The new type is far superior to the original, which emerged around 1860, and, if judiciously used for crossing, could possibly lead to the solution of the problem of crumpled silver leaves. In Improved Flower of Spring the concave leaves of the original have been replaced by flat or even convex ones. The leaf formation is not stable but this could no doubt be improved.

The hybridisation of pelargoniums has become extremely popular among amateurs, who are doing much valuable work for the progress of the genus. There were over forty entries in the "new seedling" class at the British Pelargonium Society's competition held in London in June 1972. Entries in this class had increased steadily since the formation of the society some twenty years earlier, evidence of the undoubted thrill to be experienced in the production of new hybrids entirely different from existing ones in both flower and foliage.

I have myself had great pleasure in producing golden bronzes. When growing on from the seedling stage, there was the thrill of anticipating ideal leaves; then the patient waiting for the development of the bud; and, finally, the impatient desire to see what kind of bloom would appear to accompany the lovely leaves. These types look beautiful in massed beds

Seeds germinated

and, if correctly fed, will give a stunning show of colour all summer long. Their brilliance is emphasised in dull lighting conditions. Should rain destroy the sparkling blooms, the remarkable foliage will continue to attract admiration.

Now that large flowers are available on the golden bronzes, it should follow that, in a few years' time, larger and better flowers will be hybridised on to the varieties having multi-coloured leaves; the breeding of these has really caught on and they will probably replace the normal green zonals for display purposes.

The breeding of miniatures has advanced by leaps and bounds. These beautiful plants have become a mania with collectors, many of whom are specialising in this branch exclusively. Miniatures take up less greenhouse space than do regals and zonals so that a larger number can be accommodated, adding to the pleasure of collecting them. They are now available in a vast range of form and foliage. The leaves can be green, black, silver-edged, bronze, or variegated, and some have a strong perfume; the flowers can be small or large, single or double.

If a collector of miniatures visits your greenhouse you will often see him automatically pick up a pot and remove dead leaves, if there are any. Miniatures do seem to suffer from this fault, especially when they are standing close together. The dead leaves are, fortunately, hidden behind the healthy foliage and so do not detract from the appearance—unless you are very observant—and do not hinder growth. However, it is not a bad idea to remove them periodically.

It is not at all difficult to cross-pollinate pelargoniums. Take the pollen from one pip (or floret, to use the old word), and gently put it on to the stigma in the centre of another pip. The best time to do this is when the pollen is ripe and the stigma receptive. Experience and observation will teach you when this is. Keep records of each cross. Make sure that insects do not get to the stigma before you do when it is ripe; if they do, they may insert the wrong pollen. To prevent this, cover your chosen flower with a bag made of fine-mesh netting, make your greenhouse insect-proof, or use a covered frame. Once the pollen of your choice has been accepted by the ovary at the base of the stigma, insects can no longer spoil your efforts.

I have noticed that a certain type of fly is very partial to the pollen of plants and will gobble up all that is available. This could be why some producers find certain species devoid of pollen and wrongly blame the plants. The trouble is made worse if there is a shortage of flowers for the insects to choose from.

The science of hybridisation is very bewildering: so many apparently contradictory facts have come to light. Pairs of species formerly thought to be incapable of crossing are now being crossed with the help of irradiation or chemicals such

Removing dead leaves with the aid of tweezers.

as colchicine.

The chromosome counts of many pelargonium species and present-day cultivars are much the same and these plants can be crossed if compatible. This factor is more important

Francis James, sporting

now than the changing of chromosome counts which can be done quite easily, especially with doubling. Even when the count is not known, crossing can be tried. You may get a lucky break one day, as some breeders have already done.

Wild geraniums grow all over the world. Botanists have recorded fourteen different species in the British Isles and many more in America. Some are self-fertilised, others cross-pollinated by insects. Many are naturalised by wayside and hedgerow. It is to be hoped that these flora will survive the modern advance of roadbuilding. Many of them are "protogynous", the ovary maturing before the stamens, others "homogamous", the anthers and stigma maturing simultaneously, and yet others "protandrous", the anthers maturing before the stigma is ripe.

The wild geranium *G. dalmaticum*, already mentioned in Chapter 2, is a most attractive rock plant, reaching six inches in height and smothering itself in little pink flowers in early summer. The large chunks can be divided in late summer to maintain a good supply of plants for the following year.

G. sanguinem lancastriense bears silver-pink flowers and grows four inches tall. Seed runs true to type as is usually the case with geraniums, and root cuttings can be taken.

G. pratense is one of the loveliest of these wild plants, bearing purplish-blue flowers on reddish stems.

One of the best known is *G. robertianum*. Its scent is said to be unpleasant, but this depends on your sense of smell.

G. robertianum and *G. pratense* are protandrous, *G. molle*, the "dove's foot" geranium and *G. dissectum* are homogamous, and *G. pusillan* is protogynous. Some species employ all three methods of pollination.

Can wild geraniums be crossed with the species of the pelargonium? Can either be crossed with present cultivated varieties? Not much work has been done in this field, but some backcrossing has recently been attempted by a few breeders with great success. Further efforts in this direction will probably be successful and I know personally of new cultivars emerging in this way. Wild geraniums, with their lovely foliage, present a great opportunity for hybridisers, who should keep hardiness in mind and also pay some attention to improving the present range of rock plants.

On 4 February, 1972, a scheme was laid before the British parliament for the protection of breeders' rights regarding pelargonium hybrids and genetic variants. The scheme came into operation on 25 February, 1972. It entitles a breeder to register any new cultivars with a government department, the Plant Variety Rights Office, whereafter other growers may not without his consent use the variety for propagation purposes. Any hybridiser wanting further details should write to The Plant Variety Rights Office, Murray House, Vandon Street, London S.W.1. A number of leaflets are available from this office.

The Plant Breeders' Rights Association was formed to promote the advancement of plant breeding and the exchange of information by means of meetings, lectures, discussions, publications, etc., and to advise any ministry or government department if necessary. The Association will give advice on licences and on arrangements for payment of fees and collection of royalties.

The United Kingdom is a founder member of the International Union for the Protection of New Varieties of Plants, known as UPOV. Its formation led to the International Convention for the Protection of New Varieties of Plants in 1961, signed in 1962 by the United Kingdom and subsequently ratified by Denmark, the Federal Republic of Germany, and the Netherlands.

The international Bureau for Plant Taxonomy and Nomenclature was formed in an attempt to standardise the classification and naming of plants. Various bodies throughout the world have worked with the Bureau, which has produced the International Code of Nomenclature of Cultivated Plants, a veritable mine of information; a copy of it can be obtained from the Royal Horticultural Society, London.

In my early days as a Society member, I had to think of some means of interesting the gardening public in the pelargonium. I hit on two ideas: to kill the Paul Crampel image (this plant had reigned supreme for half a century) and to play on the "geranium" misnomer as part of my campaign. More articles had to be written in the gardening press and there was a need for more books specialising on the subject. At that time, only one was available, John Crosse's "Book of the Geranium", now many years out of print.

The Paul Crampel image was easily dispelled early on as most people were keen to know more about the cultivated varieties available only from specialist pelargonium nurseries. These nurseries helped a great deal by issuing comprehensive lists, and new specialists entered the field. Most dealers in the

Francis James (ZONAL)

first half of this century sold only the Paul Crampels, the Denmarks, Henry Jacoby, Flower of Spring, Mrs. Pollock, etc. The increasing popularity of the pelargonium led to a remarkable number of new introductions in the professional growers' lists. New cultivars were being hybridised at a rapid rate.

Nurserymen's catalogues, especially those in colour, are a valuable source of knowledge. The professional specialist breeders of the past have left behind them a wealth of material whose value is not fully appreciated. Their present-day successors are constantly producing new introductions. There are no overnight fortunes to be made in this way: it is more or less a labour of love.

My publicity around the world on the misnomer question received mixed interest and was only partially successful.

It is much easier for the nurseryman to stick to the *status quo* rather than attempt to enlighten his customers on the intricate details of nomenclature, a subject which still divides the members of pelargonium societies.

Diseases and Pests

For the successful cultivation of plants, a knowledge of the various pests and diseases to which they are vulnerable is essential, all the more so if you are specialising in one particular genus. Unfortunately, pelargoniums are open to attack from a number of quarters: fungi, bacteria and viruses are among their main enemies.

It is of paramount importance to choose stock known to be free from infection, especially if it is to be used for vegetative reproduction. For the successful amateur, this selection is fairly easy due to the large number of healthy cuttings available any cutting showing the slightest sign of disease should be discarded. With some ailments, however, such as bacterial stem-rot, selection is rendered difficult by the failure of symptoms to appear until the stock has been planted out in the garden. If all diseases proclaimed their presence in a flamboyant manner, no-one would buy or use contaminated specimens and the incidence of disease would be greatly reduced. As it is, however, even honest nurserymen sometimes sell unsound plants in all innocence.

Many good, healthy varieties are being hybridised these days. The little extra spent on buying quality stock will be more than recovered by the consequent saving on fungicides, etc.

The importance of dusting cannot be overstated. Whenever you make a cut on a plant or remove a stalk or stipule, treat the wound with a fungicidal powder such as Captan; this will help to dry up the flow of sap and encourage a callus to form on the exposed surface. It will also prevent the tip of the stem or lateral from dying back which always happens when dusting is omitted.

Many of the chemicals that kill germs with great efficiency cannot be used in horticulture because they damage the plants. Carbolic acid is one example. Other compounds and the process of steam sterilisation kill off not only the harmful germs, but also the beneficial ones so that any subsequent invasion by hostile bacteria will encounter no resistance. For these reasons, chemicals used must be extremely selective in their action. Such substances are, unfortunately, few and far between.

One possibility which might be realised, given sufficient research, is the injection of beneficial predatory germs into the soil; there has recently been news of one such predator. The idea is the same as that behind penicillin and, if successful, would bring to an end the build-up in the soil of harmful chemicals. Perhaps penicillin itself, in some modified form, will prove to be the answer.

Black stem-rot, caused by the pythium fungus disease, first makes its appearance, as a rule, at the bases of cuttings set up for rooting and quickly spreads upwards. It can also occur on any part of the stem tissue. Wounds left by incisions are vulnerable to the spores and should promptly be dusted with fungicidal powder, as recommended earlier in this chapter and in Chapter 6. Many gardeners will take issue with me on this; if they do, they may change their minds through bitter experience, as was so in my case.

Botrytis blight is a very common disease, affecting mainly petals and leaves. Much can be done to prevent its spreading. During humid or rainy weather, you may see petals becoming blotchy and finally decaying; if so, take steps at once, because any rotting petal that falls on a healthy one or on a healthy leaf will infect it. The disease can spread to all parts of the plant in this way, but its progress will be arrested if you remove all marked petals and leaves, keep the foliage dry, and dust the plant with Captan or Zineb. As a rule botrytis blight is not fatal: it only disfigures the plants; if you combat the trouble promptly they will soon recover, especially if dry weather follows, when they should be given plenty of fresh air.

Remember that disease can be transmitted by air, water, instruments, insects, and hands, and plan your actions accordingly.

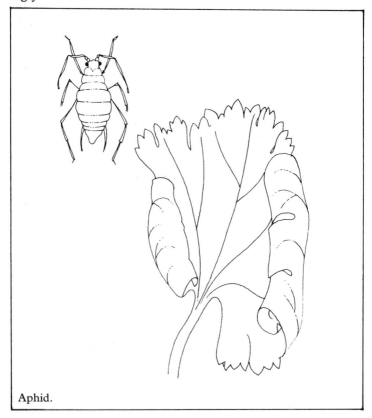

Aphid.

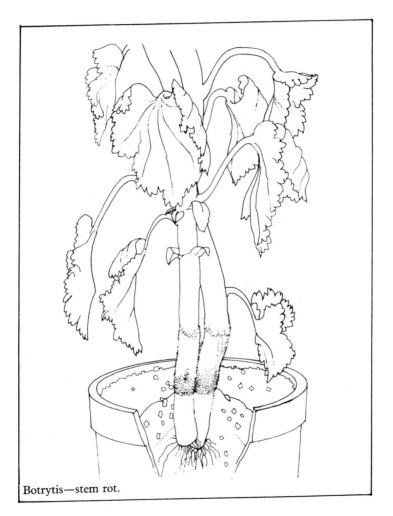

Botrytis—stem rot.

Bacterial stem-rot is the worst of all diseases because it cannot with certainty be cured by chemical or any other means. Infected plants should be burned without delay.

The disease, officially called *xanthomonas pelargonii*, was first diagnosed about a hundred years ago. The early symptoms are spots on the leaves, reminiscent of those caused by drops of water. They are usually situated underneath but can sometimes be found on the upper surfaces and grow into large yellow or brown spots, with the eventual death of the infected leaves. The bacteria spread down into the stems, turning them into unsightly dark-brown, dry, dead tissue.

If you have some very valuable stock, isolate any suspect plants as soon as infection is noticed and remove all leaves showing the slightest symptom. In this way, you may catch the disease in time before it has a chance of spreading.

The malady cannot, apparently, be inherited by a seedling from its parents but it certainly can be transmitted by vegetative propagation. The actual rot is often confined to the stem, allowing the roots to function and produce apparently healthy shoots. Do not be tempted to use these shoots for cuttings: they will almost certainly contain the germs of the disease. Rather destroy the whole plant.

A cutting in an advanced state of infection can easily be detected by the presence of a brown, cork-like piece of stem left in the compost when the cutting is lifted. With black stem-rot, the stem is slimy and comes out of the soil easily.

Attempts are being made to overcome bacterial stem-rot with "culture indexing" in the USA and "meristem tip culture" in Great Britain. These methods are quite beyond the ordinary amateur grower. They will eradicate harmful bacteria from stock but the disease-free plants, being completely sterile, will be easy prey for infection once they are planted in ordinary soil.

Leaf-spotting can be caused by a variety of diseases or by a lack of certain nutrients, making early diagnosis of bacterial stem-rot more difficult.

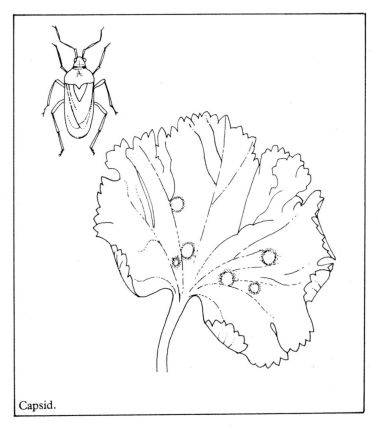

Capsid.

Sooty mould is a most disfiguring infestation which can occur at any time but is most common in autumn. It can be seen during or after an invasion of aphids. These insects suck large quantities of sap from the plant, thus weakening it.

They extract nutrient from the sap and excrete a mixture of sugar and water known as "honey-dew", one of the substances upon which ants feed. The spores of the sooty mould thrive upon the sticky surface and multiply rapidly. Regal pelargoniums are particularly liable to attack by aphids.

Treat with a sequence of fungicidal/insecticidal sprays. If the plants are not too large or in flower, immerse them in the chosen solution.

Destroy any aphids promptly, before they can multiply. This is quite easy to do—by burning nicotine shreds, for example—although the problem will probably recur.

Virus diseases do not respond to the treatment that is effective against bacteria and fungi. For complete eradication, the meristem method must be used. This is feasible only under aseptic, sterile laboratory conditions.

Viruses are tiny organisms visible only under an electron microscope. They are present in about half of the plants of the pelargonium family, and can cause vein clearing, leaf cupping, mosaic, leaf curl, etiolation, chlorosis, and malformation. Viruses can be transmitted by vegetative propagation and by aphids. Their effects are not always harmful: most infected plants grow into decent specimens. Those that show any signs of retardation or deformity should, however, be destroyed.

Mention was made, in Chapter 2, of Crocodile and White Mesh, which owe the attractive appearance of their leaves to a vein-clearing virus. The mottling seen in the foliage of many plants was caused by viruses which eventually cleared out of the variety, leaving the attractive imperfection to survive through vegetative propagation.

Rust, *puccinia pelargonii zonalis,* can cause a great deal of trouble with zonal pelargoniums as it causes defoliation. If left unchecked it can ruin an entire display, either outside or in the greenhouse. The first signs are brown spots on the upper surfaces of the leaves, accompanied on the undersides by raised reddish-brown pustules, each surrounded by a ring.

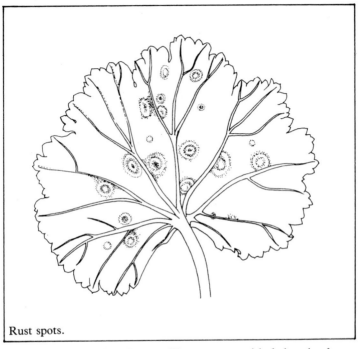

Rust spots.

In dry weather, the plants will recover unaided, but in damp conditions the disease will spread rapidly.

Zinc, a most attractive cultivar, is very vulnerable to rust and so should not be used in propagation. However, this weakness can be put to good use: the plant can be used to give early warning of the presence of the disease.

Dusting with Zineb will give a measure of control. Many chemicals have been put on the market to combat the malady, but it has adapted itself to resist one after another—much to the delight of manufacturers eager to make large profits out of novel products! The indiscriminate use of these compounds can wipe out rust's natural predators. It is only recently that the ailment has caused any real concern.

Rust can, however, be kept in check by greater attention to hygiene and correct biological control, and by the breeding of varieties resistant to the disease. Much research on the subject has been done by Miss Mary Campbell of the British Pelargonium and Geranium Society; her findings can be read in past issues of the society's journals.

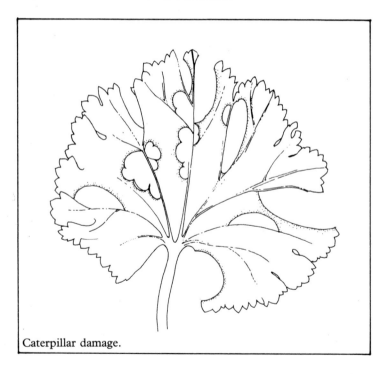

Caterpillar damage.

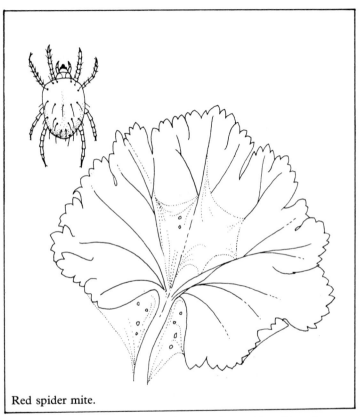

Red spider mite.

When the bottom leaves of your plants die off, make sure that they come away easily from the stem. If you break a fresh stalk away from the stem, a wound is made in living tissue, enabling germs to reach the moist flesh where they can thrive. The complete destruction of a plant by blackleg disease can come about in this way. It is much better to remove the leaf only, leaving the stalk in place. The plant will then manufacture protective tissue between the stem and the stalk; the latter, when it has died, may confidently be removed. Some may object that the dead or dying stalks detract from the appearance, but better this than to have a plant riddled with infection.

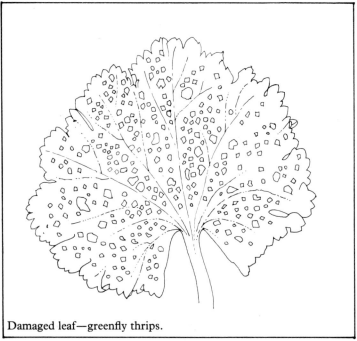

Damaged leaf—greenfly thrips.

Aphids are the insects most troublesome to pelargoniums. They can be seen as tiny dots moving on the tender shoots and multiply with great rapidity. Certain varieties of plant are more liable to attack than others and can be used to give advance warning. The pests should be eradicated as soon as they are seen. Pyrethrum, though it does not have a lasting effect, is useful against aphids if applied frequently. It is extracted from the flowers of the pyrethrum plant and kills insects by contact or when swallowed. The great advantage of this substance is its safety: it is completely harmless to humans and animals, although it must be kept away from fish.

White Chiffon

Ladybirds should be looked on as friendly insects: they do signal service in controlling the aphid population.

Caterpillars can make a sorry mess of the foliage. In England, August is the worst month for these. Jeyes Fluid keeps them away cheaply and effectively; frequent applications from a watering can will drive away not only caterpillars but, as the fluid falls on the soil, slugs and snails also. Use the compound with caution: test it on a few plants, using only half the strength recommended by the makers. If no harm results, you can try a stronger solution. Keep it off the flowers, as it can mark the petals.

Jeyes Fluid will clean up not only green-leaved plants but also many bronze- and golden-leaved ones. Do not use it in strong sunshine, especially in the greenhouse. A small quantity added to your water-butt will keep stagnation at bay.

Snails and slugs can cause very bad spoiling of the foliage on outdoor plants, though they are often wrongly blamed for damage done in fact by caterpillars and cut-worms. Treatment consists in watering foliage and soil with a solution of potassium permanganate which should be of a strong red colour if used on the ground. This will kill the useful worm population—unfortunately, except on the lawn, where the death of the worms is no bad thing.

Tomcats have a nasty habit of urinating on plants. When one such dastardly deed has been done, all the local toms will follow suit on the same plant which soon dies, much to their satisfaction. Fortunately for the pelargonium, the animals seem to favour rose bushes. Many a rose supplier has been wrongly blamed for selling poor stock, thanks to these feline escapades.

Earwigs can cause some damage. If dahlias are growing nearby, the insects attack these for preference. Canes used for staking plants constitute a convenient trap: make sure that each cane has a clear hole at the top; an earwig will hide in this during the day, ready to venture forth on destructive forays at night. Using an oil-can filled with paraffin, squirt a few drops of the liquid down a hole; out will pop the pest, when you can deal with him—if you are not squeamish—by squashing him between your fingers. Be quick to pounce, though, or he may outsmart you by tumbling to earth. Jeyes Fluid can be used in place of paraffin. Begin your offensive early in the season, before the earwigs begin to breed in a big way.

Mealy bug.

Spraying the undersides of leaves.

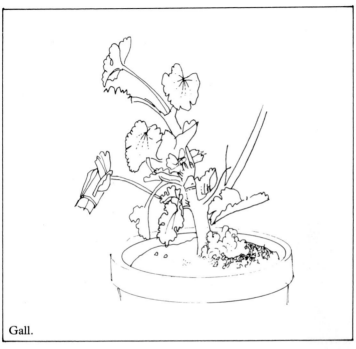

Gall.

Sparrows and many other birds should be kept out of the greenhouse. Otherwise, they will soon clear the house of the spiders so valuable as predators on pests. Robins and song-thrushes, however, should be encouraged as they help in the fight against harmful insects. One year, I would often notice a perky little robin watching me with his unflinching gaze as I went to and from my potting-shed. I began to suspect that something was afoot, and my curiosity led me to inspect the shed very carefully: tucked away on a shelf was a nest, but I did not dare to inspect it too closely. One day I returned home

77

to find several young robins flapping around the shed, unable to find the small hole through which their mother came and went. I opened a door and they soon found their way into the garden where they no doubt repaid my concern for them by setting about my enemies.

Unfortunately, if fungus disease is present, it can be spread even by our allies, the spiders and ladybirds, which should then be destroyed along with all the other insects.

Gardening journals will often help their readers with expert advice on plant ills. If you do write to them, enclose a stamped addressed envelope, as an early reply will help you to catch the trouble before it spreads. Be as specific as possible in your description of the symptoms, and enclose a few leaves and flowers whether you suspect feeding, cultivation, or disease to be at the root of the matter.

Snowbank, Carisbrook (REGALS)

May Magic (REGAL CULTIVAR)

The Geraniaceae Species

Among the genera comprising the *Geraniaceae* family are:
erodium, geranium, monsonia, pelargonium, and sarcocaulon.
They may be distinguished as follows:

(a) *Geranium* Each flower of a geranium has ten stamens
    arranged in two concentric groups of five each and all
    bear anthers. The innermost five ripen first, after which
    the five outer ones, which at the start curve widely
    outwards, ripen and move inwards by bending towards

Vivace, pansy type (ZONAL CULTIVAR)

the centre of the flower.

(b) *Pelargonium*   The flowers of pelargoniums have ten stamens but only two to seven of the stamens bear anthers; those without anthers are rudimentary. The chief characteristic which distinguishes a pelargonium is the posterior sepal with a spur, i.e. nectar-tube, which is fused with the stalk of the flower. In botanical terms the spur is said to be 'adnate' to the pedicel.

(c) *Erodium*   The flowers of the erodiums have ten stamens. The five stamens which are opposite sepals bear anthers whilst the five stamens which are opposite petals are without anthers and are rudimentary.

(d) *Monsonia*   Each flower of a monsonia has fifteen stamens all bearing anthers and arranged in five bundles of three

Eric Lee (ZONAL CULTIVAR)

each with the filaments of the stamens joined together at their bases. The central filament of each triad is longer than the others.

(e) *Sarcocaulon* The flowers of sarcocaulons have fifteen stamens and all the stamens bear anthers; all the stamens are free, being united only at their bases.

The original species constitute a most important but widely neglected subject. The fact that they are, in effect, wild plants seems to dissuade people from growing them. The pelargonium species, forebears of our modern cultivated varieties, were brought to Europe, mainly from Africa, a few centuries ago. Hybrids derived from them have recently been sent to Africa where they are much appreciated.

In this day and age we tend to spurn many things natural:

81

Carisbrook (REGAL CULTIVAR)

we go for cultivated varieties grown for direct visual sales appeal, and will not buy a plant unless it already has a few flowers on it. These flowers are achieved by treatment not always to the good of the plant if it is wanted for future use in display, and are not necessary as an indication of the plant's appearance if you buy from a reliable nurseryman.

Mr W. J. Webb, B.Sc., is one of the world's leading authorities on *Geraniaceae*. He has described many of their species. The following is a selection from Mr Webb's own writings:

Pel. alternans

"This is a sturdy and much-branched species which was introduced in 1791. Its flowers are very numerous and on a fully grown plant are white with faint reddish streaks."

Grandma Fischer (REGAL CULTIVAR)

Pel. ardens

"This beautiful hybrid was raised in 1817 by Lee of Hammersmith. It is considered to be a cross between *Pel. lobatum* and *Pel. fulgidum*. It is fairly widely distributed among collections."

Pel. aridum

"This is a very dainty member of the sub-genus of LIGULARIA. It is one of several species in the group having leaves which emit a very pleasant aromatic scent when bruised gently. The flowers are pale cream in colour."

Pel. atrum

"This species is remarkable not only for the great variability of the shape of its leaves but also in the great range in intensity of the colour of its flowers. The leaves are bristly on

83

Queen Bess (REGAL CULTIVAR)

both sides and they are carried on long petioles; their shape can be simple, pinnatifid, tripinnatifid, or pinnatipartite. The colour of the petals varies with different plants, varying from pale magenta through mahogany to almost black.

"There is a further oddity in that the same plant may have flowers of a much paler hue at different seasons in different years."

Pel. australe

"An interesting member of the PERISTERA group is *Pel. australe*. This species is widely distributed and several forms are found in Australia and one in Tasmania. Each of the islands between Australia and Tasmania seems to have its own particular variety of *Pel. australe*."

Maréchal Macmahon (GOLDEN BRONZE CULTIVAR)

Pel. betulinum
"This species was introduced into this country in 1786; it has attractive flowers and foliage. The leaves are not unlike beech leaves: hence the name. The leaves are lemon-scented. Both white- and purple-flowered varieties are known."

Pel. bowkeri
"This species, which was introduced in 1863, is a very interesting subject. The mature leaves are of a beautiful grey-green colour and are very much divided, which imparts a soft fern-like appearance to the plant. The leaves produced by young tubers are triangular in shape with few lobes but the leaves produced from mature tubers are long and pinnate throughout their length. Individual leaves thus differ most

85

Singlewell (REGAL CULTIVAR)

considerably with the age of the tuber. The flowers have a most bizarre appearance, the petals being very deeply cut with long fringes. The upper petals are of a greenish yellow colour with bright purple veinings. The lower petals are purplish in hue. The scent is unpleasant. Altogether it is one of those flowers which only their own mothers could love. The species is found in Natal and the Orange Free State."

Pel. carnosum
"This is a very well known species. It was introduced into the U.K. in 1724 and is characterised by its thick, succulent stems with few branches. Its leaves are oblong and pinnate but sometimes pinnatifid. It flowers well and is distinguished by the rounded or spoon-shaped ends to its flower petals

Prince Olaf (REGAL CULTIVAR)

whereas other species in this sub-genus have petal ends that are rather more pointed. There are other differences, of course, which are to be noted on closer inspection. I have found that the seeds of this species are some of the quickest to germinate: seeds have been known to do so in under three days. The flowers have a delicate, sweet scent in warm sunshine, which makes the plant rather attractive."

Pel. cordatum
   "This is an attractive species in the PELARGIUM group. Like many of its relatives, it makes a handsome plant."

Pel. cotyledonis
   "This species, which is reported to be found on the Island of St. Helena, has a number of curious characteristics. The

Annie Hawkins (REGAL CULTIVAR)

species has thick, succulent stems which become woody with age and the leaves, which sprout in tufts from the tips of the stems, are attached by their centres to their petioles, instead of the more usual edge attachment. In this way the leaves resemble the leaves of *Pel. peltatum*. The flowers are of a beautiful, translucent white and the five petals, being regularly shaped, form a delicate chalice.''

Pel. crassicaule
"This is a very succulent species introduced in 1785. The stipules of this species are not so very conspicuous as is usually the case with other members of the sub-genus CORTUSINA. It is, however, easily distinguished from other species by its thick brown stems and by the way in which the leaf blades taper into

Queen Hermione (REGAL)

the petiole. The flowers are very freely produced and are white with tiny red spots. After acclimatisation, the plant usually flowers around the turn of the year, and so makes a welcome change from the bare, leafless appearance of a number of the species in this sub-genus at this time."

Pel. echinatum

"The best-known species in the sub-genus CORTUSINA is *Pel. echinatum* or the 'Sweetheart' pelargonium, so called from the heart-shaped markings on its petals. Even the bee markings have a fanciful resemblance to kisses. It has been known since 1794."

Pel. endlicherianum

"This species, which was introduced in 1842, is unique as

Aztec (REGAL CULTIVAR)

it is the only known hardy species. It hails from Asia Minor. Although it is said to be hardy it does not seem to like our winters and it requires some protection to shelter it from too much rain."

Pel. frutetorum
"A relative newcomer to the sub-genus CICONIUM being introduced only in 1932. It is a very graceful and attractive species although rather inclined to straggle if not supported." Several beautiful hybrids of this species have been bred in the past few years, especially by Miss Mary Campbell. These hybrids will become extremely popular in the coming years.

Pel. fulgidum
"A deciduous species introduced in 1732, well known for the

Blythwood (REGAL CULTIVAR)

intense vermilion colour of its petals. It is also noted for the very large size of its nectar tube, one of the largest to be observed."

Pel. gibbosum
"This is a popular species and one which is most frequently found in general collections of pelargonium species. Flowering plants vary in height between ten and thirty inches. When its stems are young they are succulent but become woody with increasing age. The plant has relatively few stems. These stems are smooth (hairless) and are much thicker at their nodes than midways. This gives the stems a gouty appearance and it is on account of this feature that the species receives its name. The leaf-blades are thin, almost papery in substance,

Rapture (REGAL CULTIVAR)

grey-green in colour, and covered with a fine bloom like that seen on a cabbage leaf. The leaves are practically hairless and they are pinnately lobed almost to the mid-rib. The leaves have two lower lobes which are cut to the mid-rib and almost stalkless. The leaf-edges are toothed. The flower-heads bear 5–10 flowers. The flowers are almost stalkless but have very long adnate spurs giving the appearance of long stalks. The flower petals are small, the two upper ones being slightly larger than the three lower ones; the colour of the petals is a uniform, dingy, greenish yellow. The natural habitat is the south-western area of Cape Province. It is also found in the south-western coastal areas. The species was first introduced in 1712."

L'Elégante (IVY CULTIVAR)

Pel. hirtum

"This species, which was introduced in 1790, is low growing and passes the summer in a dormant state. In the Fall, however, it puts on a clothing of feathery green leaves to be followed by flowers in the early spring. The leaves are bright green in colour and bear tufts of pinnae accounting for the feather-like appearance. The flowers are of a rich rosy-violet colour. It can be easily raised from seeds which generally germinate in two to three weeks."

Pel. linearipetalum

"This is a very attractive tuberous-rooted species in the HOAREA sub-genus. It is found in the south-western area of Cape Province, and the west coast regions of South Africa.

The plant's leaves are very variable in shape: those which are first produced, viz.. those at the base, are entire with a stalk (petiole) about as long as the leaf-blade itself; the leaves produced later are almost stalkless and held depressed to the ground, hence the alternative name of *Pel. depressum (Jacq)*.

"Under cultivation, the leaves usually wither away before the flowers expand. The plant is stemless. The flowering stalk is between five and six inches high. Individual blossoms are relatively large for so small a plant, being about one and three-quarter inches across. The petals are linear, being extremely long and narrow, and are constantly on the move in the slightest breeze. The petals are of a delicate, pretty shade of pale pink with bright carmine veining in the lower half of each of the two upper petals, giving the impression of dainty ribbons fluttering in the air currents. In common with other tuberous-rooted species, it seems to be moderately hardy. After flowering, the plant dies down completely, but when the turn of the year is past and the days are lengthening the plant springs up again to repeat its growth cycle."

Pel. pinnatum

"This is a tuberous-rooted species which was first introduced into Britain in 1801. Its natural habitat is the south-western area of Cape Province near Cape Town.

"The leaves of the species have long, slender leaf-stalks bearing a variable number of ovate or roundish leaflets (pinnae). These leaflets occur alternatively or almost opposite one another on each side of a common leaf-stalk, and all leaflets and stalks are covered with fairly coarse, stiff, long, straight hairs. The number of leaflets on each leaf-stalk is very variable: those leaves which are the first produced often have a single leaflet at their tips, but for those which are developed later the number increases with each leaf. Sometimes there are as many as fifteen leaflets on one stalk, and occasionally even more. The flowering stems are branching and covered with fine, soft hairs. The umbels are compound and each head is many-

Godfrey's Pride (REGAL)

flowered. The colour of the petals is white, yellow, or flesh coloured and the petals are marked with a fine veining of deeper colour. The two upper petals are also marked with dark red-purple spots at their bases. This is a very attractive species and is not difficult to grow. In England it flowers in early spring, which makes it a very welcome sight in the greenhouse."

Pel. radula

"This species, which was introduced into Britain in 1774 by Francis Masson, is an erect-branching, shrubby plant growing about three feet high. Its stems are slender and bear many leaves, which are triangular in shape. The shape of the leaves is described as pinnatipartite with pinnatifid segments. The upper

A Campbell miniature

surfaces of the leaves are covered with fairly coarse, stiff, long, erect hairs. An important characteristic of the leaves is the rolling of the under edges. The leaves are very pleasantly scented, the scent being described by some as similar to that of a rose; the scent, however, is not given off until the leaves are gently bruised. The flower stems are short and generally there are only five flowers per umbel. The petals are pink in colour, the two upper petals being longer and broader than the three lower ones, and they are also veined and spotted with purple. The shape of the upper petals is obovate, i.e. they have the broadest part above the mid-section; the ratio of length to breadth is about three to two. The natural habitat of the species is S.W. Cape Province, S. Africa. It is a fairly common species, being found often in the ruts of rough tracks."

Russell Viner (MINIATURE)

Pel. rapaceum

"This is one of the most beautiful of all the pelargonium species.

"It is characterised by a large, carrot-shaped rootstock which lies entirely below the ground. From two to three heads are formed on the tuber depending on the age of the tuber. The leaves which appear from the tops of these heads in tufts are variable. They are long and linear from six to nine inches long and much dissected, and are softly hairy. It is in its flowers that the main beauty of the species lies as well as its strangeness. The two upper petals are narrow and strongly reflexed about halfway along their length. The three lower petals are broad and held straight out, entirely enclosing the anthers much in the manner of the petals of a sweet pea. In

97

the bud stage, individual flowers appear as if there will be two distinct blossoms and it is most interesting to watch the expansion of the petals, for the deception is kept up for some time. Three varieties of the species are recognised: one called *var. selinum*, has whitish- to flesh-coloured petals; another, called *var. luteum*, has yellow petals, and the third, called *var. cordalifolia*, has primrose yellow petals and has leaves which bear leaflets which are much more dissected than those of the first two varieties mentioned. In its natural habitat, which is the Cape Province, it flowers at any time from spring to throughout the summer. It is fairly common and it is said that the baboons in the area dig up the tubers for food. Being a tuberous species it is fairly hardy."

Pel. spinosum

"This species, which was introduced in 1796, is one of particular interest. It is a much branched, shrubby species, easily recognised by its long leaf-stalks or petioles, three to four inches in length and terminating in bright-green, glossy leaves. Both the stipules and the petioles harden into spines which persist and form the characteristic by which the species can be readily identified. The leaves have a peculiar, pungent scent when they are bruised. It is a Namaqualand species and is more or less confined to altitudes higher than 3,400 feet. It flowers in late September in South Africa, shortly after the rains have fallen. The flowers are whitish in colour with a rosy patch in the mid-zone of the petals, with veinings of stronger colour.

"The flowers have five stamens. It is rather a fussy species, requiring careful attention to its environmental surroundings in cultivation."

Pel. sulphureum

"This very attractive species is a member of this sub-genus. It is noteworthy for the yellow colour of its flowers, for yellow is a colour not usually found among Pelargoniums. Yet another strange feature of its flowers is that they usually

Topper (ZONAL)

have only two fertile stamens. Sometimes there is only one fertile stamen, but the seed that results is quite healthy. One very noticeable characteristic of this species is that its leaves are practically entire in outline (i.e., there are no notches or lobes) and that the leaves form a rosette lying close to the ground somewhat after the habit of a primula. When in full growth, the plant produces a number of flowering trusses in succession and may be in bloom from early September to January, but the exact flowering time is rather unpredictable. It has a long resting period when its leaves shrivel up and all one has is a dull and apparently lifeless tuber. Seed sets quite freely and usually germinates in three to seven weeks. The plant, which was introduced into the U.K. around 1907, is found near the Hex River in South-West Cape Province."

99

Pel. tabulare

"The first introduction of this species into Britain was by Francis Masson in 1775. It is a small herbaceous shrub, very much branched and growing from six to eight inches high. Individual plants are relatively short-lived, in cultivation living from two to three years only, but fortunately the plants usually produce an abundance of seed without any difficulty so that their survival is well provided for. It has thin, hairy, erect stems in its early growth, but older plants tend to sprawl later. The leaves are produced alternately on the stems, and the leaf-blades, which are carried on long, thin stalks, are often zoned. The leaf-blades are five- to seven-lobed and their edges are marked with sharply pointed teeth. The flower-stalks carry from one to four flowers; the colour of the flower-petals is pale yellow. The petals are held horizontally: hence the name 'tabulare'. *Pel. tabulare* can easily be confused with *Pel. saniculaefolium* but a comparison of leaf shapes and flower shape and colour will quickly distinguish them. The sides of the lobes of the leaves of *Pel. tabulare* are rounder than those of *Pel. saniculaefolium* and the flowers of the latter are pink in colour whereas, as already mentioned, the former has pale-yellow flowers. Altogether, *Pel. tabulare* is a very dainty plant; its bright-green, purple-zoned, leaves and unusually shaped pale-yellow flowers make it most attractive."

Pel. tetragonum

"This species, which was introduced in 1774, is very well known. It is easily propagated by cuttings. When out of flower, the plant presents a rather stark appearance but it makes up for this when in bloom for its flowers are large and showy and very handsome. The flowers are usually produced in pairs. There are several varieties with flowers of varying shades of purple."

Pel. triste

"*Pel. triste* is one of the species included in the sub-genus of POLYACTIUM. The name Polyactium is in reference to the ray-

Violarium tricolour (SPECIES). There are several varieties.

like appearance of the many flowers contained in each of the umbels produced by the species in the group, most of which have night-scented flowers.

"In general the scent is sweet rather like musk or ginger-bread but the scent of the flowers of some species is most unpleasant. The members of the group have tuberous roots or thick underground stems and nearly all are deciduous. Their leaves are lobed or pinnately divided and as already mentioned their umbels carry many flowers. The individual flowers are long-spurred and are almost sessile and they have seven fertile stamens."

Pel. violarium
"This species with its striking two-colour flowers and its

most beautifully shaped leaves of a greyish-green colour always presents a graceful appearance. The species is said to have been introduced in 1792 and specimens are to be found in most collections."

The following information has been sent in to me by Mr Nic. Jooste of the South African Pelargonium and Geranium Society. He has considerable personal knowledge of the pelargonium species. The flowering periods mentioned are those obtaining in South Africa:

Pel. bechuanicum

"A much-branched shrub about one foot high with dissected leaves like carrot leaves. Grows mainly in the Transvaal highlands and Botswana. Flowers are small and white in colour. There are only four petals to a bloom, with the upper two petals broader than the lower two. Flowers from spring to autumn. *Bechuanicum* grows in medium, well-drained soil and can stand a certain amount of cold. Grows in full sun."

Pel. bechuanicum var. latisectum

"Perennial herb up to one and a-half feet high, freely branched from the base, with dissected leaves. Leaves larger than those of *bechuanicum* and root-stock rather thick. Flower small, four petals as in *bechuanicum* and light pink in colour. Flowers from spring to mid-summer. *Var. latisectum* likes the same conditions and is found in the Transvaal highlands."

Pel. capitatum

"A soft-wooded, straggling plant. Abundant on sand dunes and low hillsides near sea. Leaves are velvety and sweet-scented when bruised. The flowers are borne in dense umbels and are pink and dark-veined. The flowering period is from spring to autumn. Likes well-drained, medium soil. The roots must be in the shade with branches in full sun. In nature, it grows in bushes with branches penetrating out. It likes a certain amount of humidity."

Pel. capullatum

"A tall shrub, growing up to eight feet high. Sometimes called the "tree pelargonium". Stems are soft and succulent when young, becoming woody with age. Leaves are up to six inches across, simple in form, and hairy. The flowers are borne in an umbel, clear bright-mauve, upper two petals broader and heavily marked with magenta veins. Grows on the Cape Peninsula. Likes well drained, rich soil and grows better in semi-shade. Flowers in spring only. It is hardy and requires plenty of water from spring to autumn. Let soil dry out completely before watering again. During winter, water only once a week."

Pel. echinatum

"A very succulent shrub with a thick stem, covered with prickles; very few branches. Leaves are simple, closely spaced, dark-green, hairy beneath, and velvety above. The flowers are borne in an umbel, the white flowers marked and veined in crimson. A pink form can also be found. The species grows in the Eastern Cape and Natal Mountains; it likes sandy, slightly acid soil and semi-shade. Also to be found in Namaqualand. The flowering period is from spring to autumn. As it is succulent, water once a week during the flowering period and once a month during winter."

Pel. graveolens

"A densely tufted shrub. The branches are soft when young, becoming hard with age. The leaves are deeply lobed. The plant grows on south-facing stony slopes in the Grahamstown district of the Eastern Cape Province. The flower is purple in colour and deeply veined. The plant flowers in spring. Likes well-drained soil and grows in full sun on the cold-facing sides of mountains."

Pel. graveolens "Mores Victory"

"This is a hybrid of *Pel. graveolens.* The flower is deep red; the plant flowers all the year round when protected from frost."

Pel. hybridum (salmoneum)

"An evergreen bush with a slender stem growing about two to three feet high. The leaves are yellowish brown, scalloped, and hairy above. The flower is salmon-coloured and very sparse on umbel. Likes a sandy but not too rich soil and grows in the Eastern Cape around Port Elizabeth. Water well in summer period and let soil dry out before watering again. During winter, water sparingly. Likes full sun, and flowers during spring and autumn."

Pel. inquinans

"A soft, woody, well-shaped shrub growing up to two feet high. The branches are round and soft when young with dense, short hairs becoming hard with age. The leaves are simple, shortly pubescent, and velvety. The plant flowers all

Pandora (ZONAL)

the year round, the flowers being scarlet and borne in an umbel; it grows inland in the Eastern Cape Province. The plant grows better in filtered condition, in well-drained acid soil. It should only be watered when completely dry."

Pel. myrrhifolium
"This is a low-growing shrub of trailing habit, about six inches tall. The semi-succulent stem becomes woody with age. Leaves are about two inches long, ovate-oblong and more or less deeply pinnated. The flowering period is from spring to autumn; the flowers, pale mauve-pink, are borne in umbels of two to six flowers. The plant grows around Cape Town in the Western Cape Province. It likes a sandy but not too rich soil, slightly acid, and grows well under shrubs. It requires watering in winter with very little during summer."

Pel. peltatum
"A rambling plant which becomes woody at base with age. The leaves are fleshy and evergreen with five points and measure about two inches across. The flower is pale pink or lilac with magenta markings on the upper two petals. The flowering period is from spring to autumn and the plant can be found in Eastern Cape Province up to the southern part of Natal. Likes well-drained, slightly acid soil. Requires plenty of watering during flowering period, less during winter. The plant likes to grow in full sun and next to shrubs."

Pel. reniforme
"This grows inland in Eastern Cape Province on open flats and grassland. Rootstock is large and woody. The leaves are simple, closely spaced and greyish green. The flowers are small with about ten blooms in a loose umbel, borne in profusion, and brilliant cerise in colour. It flowers all the year round and grows in well-drained, slightly acid soil, in full sun."

Pel. zonale
"An evergreen shrub, semi-succulent, growing about three feet tall. Stem gets woody with age. Leaves are simple with a

dark purplish brown band or zone. Size of leaves: about three inches across. The flowers are borne in an umbel and can be found in pink shading to white. *Zonale* grows in the northern part of Eastern Cape Province right up to and including Natal. It grows in full sun, in well-drained medium soil, and needs watering well during the flowering period of spring to autumn. It flowers during the winter period also, but to a lesser extent."

Hybrids bred by Henry J. Wood

ANDREA DARWIN	Large single red. Deep zone on leaves.
ALLURING	Pale pink single flower, dark zone on leaf. A pretty plant.
AMBITION	From Eric Lee. Deep red.
BARBARA CLARK	A golden bronze with a large single pink flower. A good bedder which likes plenty of sun and weather.
CLEAR POND	Very large single deep pink. Faint zone.
EDEN PARK	Pure white flower that does not shatter.
ENDLESS JOY	A *frutetorum*. Single scarlet, medium head, crinkly leaves; very vigorous.
ETHEL JAMES	A seedling from Francis James. Very large single pink flower that does not shatter easily, therefore good for showing. Almost a bi-colour at times.
GOLDEN ATOM	Similar to Barbara Clark but with a red single flower in complete harmony with the golden foliage.

GOLDEN CENTRE	Deep red single, golden bronze foliage.
GOLDEN CHIEF	Large single red; golden bronze foliage with deep zone.
GOLDEN EARTH	From Golden Atom. Small florets, grand golden bronze foliage.
GOLDEN MOON	Single pink flower, golden bronze with deep zone.
GOLDEN PEACE	From Golden Atom. Large red flower on golden bronze leaves.
GOLDEN SANDS	Deep red single flower, golden leaves.
GOLD SOVEREIGN	Small double red flower with bright golden bronze leaves. Foliage very good and stands out well in bad weather. Propagates easily.
GOLF BALL	From Eric Lee. Large single pink flower.
GOOD TIDINGS	Large single pink.
HENRY JAMES	Similar to Ethel James, but a deeper shade of pink.
LILLIAN WOOD	Single pink. Medium-sized plant.
PATRICA DARWIN	A *frutetorum*. Large double pink flower that does not shatter. Crinkly leaves.
PEACE CRUSADE	Very large white-flushed pink.
PINK RIBBONS	Very powerful large single pink, large pips.
PINK TRICKS	Large pink single, large pips, very large head, deep zone; extremely good.
RED BANK	Partly gold leaf, large red flower. From Eric Lee. Should be a great grower.

RED JAMES	Single red flower. Sport from Francis James.
SILENT OAF	Deep red single. Large flower. Very vigorous grower.
SUMMER FRESHNESS	A *frutetorum*. Very vigorous. Pale pink flower, semi-double. Crinkly leaves.
UNSPOILT	Lovely shade of pink. Medium grower. Good bedder.
YOURS TRULY	Extremely powerful grower with very wide deep zone. Deep pink single flower, small pips. Medium head.

Dwarfs

EDEN PARK	Pure white that does not shatter.
JEAN BETTY	Double white.

Miniatures

RED BIRD	Red single, dark foliage
RED BUNNY	Red single, dark foliage
RUSSELL VINER	Pink single, dark foliage
SUSAN BROOK	Pink single, dark foliage.
WILLIAM WOOD	A very lovely pink single, dark foliage.

Wood Introductions

ERIC LEE	A very large magenta with over 120 pips in the head.
IMPROVED FLOWER OF SPRING	Should never be mixed with the original because of the great improvement.

To get the best definition for the classification of pelargonium cultivars one has to turn to the list published in the British Pelargonium and Geranium Society's year book of 1957. This is given in the Preamble on page 22, and is arranged as follows:

Zonal pelargoniums.

ZONAL PELARGONIUMS
Single-flowered group, having normally no more than five petals.

Double- and semi-double-flowered group, having flowers normally composed of six or more petals but not hearted like the bud of a rose.

Rosebud group, fully double and hearted, the middle petals remaining unopened like the bud of a rose.

Cactus-flowering group, petals twisted into quills.

Fancy-leaved group, silver-leaved; silver tricolours; golden-leaved; bronze and gold; black-leaved; butterfly-leaved; golden tricolours.

Dwarf group.

Miniature group

REGAL PELARGONIUMS.

IVY-LEAVED PELARGONIUMS.

HYBRID IVY-LEAVED PELARGONIUMS.

SCENTED-LEAVED PELARGONIUMS.

UNIQUE PELARGONIUMS.

ANGLE PELARGONIUMS.

Selected Lists of Well-tried Varieties

Single-flowered group

Barbara Bennett, pink; Barbara Hope, carmine; Belvedere Glory, pink; Block, scarlet; Bruce, white; Brutus, vermilion; Christmas Sun, orange; Countess of Jersey, red; Doris Moore, cherry; Eden Perfection, salmon; Ethel James, pink; Francis James, pink bi-colour; Golden Lion, pink; Grenadier, vermilion; Henry Jacoby, red; Henry James, deep pink; Jane Campbell, orange; Kingswood, carmine; Lady Warwick, picotee; Mauretania, white centre, ringed, camellia; Maxim Kovalevski, vermilion; Mrs. E. G. Hill, rose; Mrs. R. Thompson, red; Nottinghill Beauty, rose; Pride

of the West, rose; Salmon Kovalevski, rose; Topper, rose;
Vera Dillon, magenta; Victorious, vermilion; Victory, rose;
Winter White, white.

Double- and semi-double-flowered group
Countess of Albemarle, rose; Dagata, rose; Dodd's Super
Double, cherry; Double Jacoby, crimson; Edmund Lachenal,
red; Forest Maid, pink; Garibaldi, rose; Genetrix, rose;
Gustav Emich, red; Hermione, white; Improved Rickard,
red; Irenes, most varieties; Jean Oberle, pink; Jewel,
rose; King Fiat, coral salmon; King of Denmark, salmon;
Monsieur Emil David, purple; Mrs. Lawrence, pink;
Orange Sonne, orange; President Baillet, red; Princess
Fiat, salmon and white; Queen Fiat, salmon; Royal Fiat,
pink; Royal Purple, magenta; Zonnekind, pink.
The coloured-leaved group contains the most beautiful
plants we have in the family of *Geraniaceae*. I have made this
section as comprehensive as I possibly can because these
plants have a tremendous future for both pot work in the greenhouse and, especially, outside garden display, where they will
give of their best. Most like plenty of sun.

The advantage of coloured leaves in the garden is greatly in
evidence when the weather is very wet, causing damping off
of the blooms. When this occurs, the lovely colours in the
foliage of the plants will take over the brilliant display, so
making the loss of colour of the fading blooms less obvious.

There should be a big increase in the number of these lovely
varieties in the coming years because of their great popularity
with growers and breeders, especially with the production of
better flowers of all colours; more white flowers are needed,
however.

You must not overdo the use of Epsom salts or potash on
plants in this section, especially on those having multi-
coloured leaves, such as Dolly Varden, Henry Cox, and the
golden bronzes like Gaiety Girl. Otherwise the leaves will
lose their lovely colours and eventually die.

Golden bronze leaves

Barbara Clark, large single pink; Bronze Corinne, vermilion; Bronze Queen, single red; Copper Flair, single salmon; Dollar Princess, single pink; Gaiety Girl, single pink; Golden Atom, large single scarlet; Golden Fleece, double pink; Golden Masterpiece, double rose; Golden Orfe, single rose; Gold Sovereign, double scarlet; Maréchal Mac Mahon, single red; Mrs. Quilter, single salmon.

Golden leaves

Golden Crest, single red; Golden Harry Hieover, single scarlet; Golden Sand, single red; Robert Fish, single vermilion; Verona, single pink.

Bi-coloured leaves

A Happy Thought, single crimson; Caroline Schmidt, double red; Crystal Palace Gem, single rose; Distinction, single red; Flower of Spring, single vermilion; Freak of Nature, small single vermilion; King of the Boars, single salmon; Madam Butterfly, double crimson; Madam Salleron, no flower; Mangles Variegated, single red; Medallion, single salmon; Mrs. Mappin, single white, vermilion centre; Mrs. Parker, double pink; Pink Happy Thought, single; Sea Nymph, wide zone.

Multi-coloured leaves

Dolly Varden; Henry Cox; Lass o' Gowrie; Miss Burdett Coutts; Mrs. Pollock; Peter Grieve; Sophie Dumaresque. All of these have small flowers.

Under the above headings I have given the names of cultivars which I know from personal experience to be worthwhile varieties to grow in the greenhouse or garden. If a cultivar has not been mentioned here, it does not necessarily mean that it is not a good one. The check list of the British Pelargonium and Geranium Society will give you a greater selection.

Prince Regent (GOLDEN LEAF)

Societies and Their Work

After thirty years' membership of many horticultural societies, I have come to the conclusion that such organisations are of vital importance to plant- and flower-lovers. The societies increase their members' knowledge through lectures, talks, meetings, outings, and, above all, shows. They represent excellent value for money: the subscriptions charged are so small that they do not even cover expenses and must be supplemented by the proceeds of raffles, bring-and-buy stalls, the sale of literature, and other fund-raising efforts. These are generally run by a hard core of enthusiasts who, together with the working committee members, form the backbone of the societies and, indeed, derive the greatest enjoyment from them. Increases in postal charges and costs generally have hit the societies very hard; this state of affairs is likely to continue. It is all too easy for people to economise by cutting out their subscriptions. When increasing costs force corresponding rises in subscription rates—in order to keep a society solvent—many members resent the extra sums involved and cease to subscribe, unless they are very keen specialists. This is a pity, considering the pleasure that these societies give to their members.

If you are thinking of forming a society of specialist pelargonium enthusiasts, gather a group of willing people together to thrash out a constitution setting forth its aims. The general purpose should, of course, be the cultivation of *Geraniaceae*. Rules should be written, within the constitution or otherwise, but these should be kept simple since no-one likes to be bogged down in a morass of clauses, articles, sections, and so forth. The purpose of rules is to achieve good fellowship and harmony among members.

Officers should be elected to carry out the various tasks necessary to the smooth running of the society. Success will be achieved through close team-work and acceptance of majority decisions by the officers of the council or committee, not through domination by one person or a small clique—although occasionally there are exceptions.

A society is only as good as its members make it. Lack of interest and too much dissent will make it disintegrate.

Always remember that the society has been set up to promote the cultivation of plants. Shows and exhibitions are the most important events in the calendar, as they enable the general public to see what can be done. If trial grounds can be maintained, so much the better. The value of exhibitions is indicated by the large attendances at Chelsea, Southport, and the county shows.

The more countries with specialist societies the better. All existing societies co-operate internationally, with much useful exchange of information. This must lead to greater interest on the part of the gardening public in both pelargoniums and geraniums. I should be pleased to hear from keen growers in countries where no pelargonium societies exist and should gladly offer help in the formation of such.

As an indication of the increasing popularity of pot plants, many new combined pelargonium and fuchsia societies are being formed, having affiliations with the B.P.G.S. and the B.F.S.

In general horticultural shows, pot plants are making up a considerable proportion of the entries received. This should be encouraged, as pot plant classes could replace the many flower classes that are being poorly supported at present.

The British Pelargonium and Geranium Society offers certificates and other awards to affiliated societies in the hope of encouraging pelargonium-growing at local level. It also runs a special class for these societies in its annual competition in London. Particulars are available from the Hon. Secretary.

The British Pelargonium and Geranium Society

The specialist horticultural society which has made the greatest impact on the gardening world during the past twenty years is the British Pelargonium and Geranium Society. Without its aid, the pelargonium could not have gained the popularity it presently enjoys in the United Kingdom. The work has all been done on an honorary basis by council and ordinary members, who have helped to spread information about a plant whose vast potential has not yet been matched by sufficient knowledge, among the gardening public, of the facts pertaining to it.

The society was formed in 1951 under the title of "The Geranium Society". Several years later, when the council became more aware of correct nomenclature, its name was changed to its present form, although many members still dissent.

Ever since the society was started, it has tried to put some order into the jumble of names in current use—an almost impossible task since the same variety can appear under different names in different nurserymen's lists; this failing is more rampant in Britain than overseas. A certain degree of success was achieved in 1970 when the society published its first check list of cultivated varieties. Although very far from complete, it is undoubtedly a foretaste of bigger things to come, especially with the co-operation of overseas societies that is now taking place. The list was published in an attractive loose cover and was so arranged that additions and amendments could be made when necessary. It can be bought on application to the society's Secretary.

Many B.P.G.S. members started breeding new varieties and have achieved great success, especially with miniatures and dwarf plants. When the society was formed, only about ten miniature, and no dwarf, pelargoniums were to be found in specialist catalogues. This situation has now been vastly improved.

The plant has been promoted in a stand run by the society at the big Chelsea show for the last eight years. In addition, the society holds a competition each June in the Royal Horticultural Society's hall in London; hundreds of first-class plants are entered each year, giving the gardening public some idea of the huge range available.

Many years ago, the country was split into regions, each subdivided into groups, in an endeavour to promote the pelargonium at local level. This has met with moderate success.

The B.P.G.S. has published a year book and three journals annually, containing articles of interest to, and written by, members. There is plenty of scope here for budding authors! The cost of these periodicals is only just covered by subscriptions: additional income has to be found, for example

Barbara Hope (ZONAL)

the proceeds from book sales and donations from generous members.

At the society's first conference, held at Syon House in 1970, a most important paper was read by Mr W. J. Webb, who illustrated his lecture with slides. The paper was published in the society's 1971 year book, which can be obtained from the Hon. Secretary. Other speakers were Mr R. A. Stephenson and Miss E. J. Willson.

The second conference was held at the Berrow Court Hotel, Birmingham. The speakers were Mrs Monica Bennett, Miss E. J. Willson, and Mr W. G. Rutter of Birmingham University. The speeches were followed by a brains trust. An excellent dinner was served, and the whole occasion was one of the most enjoyable in the history of the society, an encouragement to the council to hold many more such useful events at various venues.

Enquiries may be addressed to the Hon. Secretary at: 129 Aylesford Avenue, Beckenham, Kent, England.

The International Geranium Society

The second specialist geranium society to be formed in this century was the American Pelargonium Society, which later changed its name to the International Geranium Society. There is no doubt that the Americans have played a leading part in bringing the plant into prominence. At the time the society was formed, specialist nurserymen in the States were selling literally millions of plants every year, in line with their intensive breeding campaign.

The first printed journal of the society was published in August/September 1953. There are four every year, and they are noted for the remarkable cover illustrations, a feature that has been maintained from the first issue right up to the present. Many of the journals can still be obtained by application to the Membership Secretary.

Like the members of Australian societies, the Americans have to travel long distances by air to get to conferences and directors' meetings but this does not seem to deter them.

From the beginning, the society has put a great deal of hard work into trying to sort out the taxonomy of the plant, and has met with some success. The latest news is that it has published the "Spalding List". To quote from the society's April 1972 journal:

"The Spalding List is a file of about 7,000 cards, the four-year monumental task of George Spalding, former President of I.G.S., and his mother Mrs Spalding. This historical list includes the names of Pelargoniums and all available information about them, from very old records up to the early 1960's."

A group of I.G.S. members has financed the typing of data from the cards on to standard letter-size paper and then the

Delight (ZONAL)

mimeographing of numerous copies. This was accomplished by advance payment for lists.

The list will cover about 350 pages, at a cost of $10 per list. If other members, breeders, introducers, or nurseries want copies, a few extra lists are available.

For each list, a bill (American) for $10 plus one dollar to cover mailing should be sent to: Miss Francis Hartsook, 5017 North Ecinita Ave., Temple City, California 91780, U.S.A.

Miss Hartsook is a well-known hybridist in America and has been responsible for many lovely introductions.

The South African Pelargonium and Geranium Society

This society is of great importance, as most of the pelargonium species are indigenous to South Africa. It publishes journals every March, June, September, and December. These are of unique interest in that they contain articles written by members having direct access to the plants in their natural habitat. Members of the society have carried out a great deal of research, and there is no doubt that they have aroused much interest in the species, of which between 250 and 300 have been recorded, most unobtainable by the average collector.

Very little in the way of hybridisation has been done in South Africa, so that cultivated hybrids from England and the U.S.A. are much sought after there. Supplies go out from time to time by air, but the rapid reversal of climate has an adverse effect, causing some losses.

The Hon. Secretary of the South African P.G.S. is Mrs J. de Villiers, P.O. Box 74, Muldersdrift, Transvaal, South Africa.

The Australian Societies

The first conference of Australian pelargonium and geranium societies was held in Adelaide in October, 1971, and chaired by Mr Robert F. G. Swinbourne, F.L.S. Not all of the societies were represented. The aims adopted were: to achieve harmony among the existing Australian societies; to bring credit and publicity to the plant; and to strive for uniformity in nomenclature, judging standards, etc.

It was agreed to publish 800 copies of a year book. This has now been issued. It contains a number of contributions from people in various parts of the world and hence has international importance; among these are a very comprehensive article on pelargonium species, by Mr W. J. Webb, B.Sc., of the B.P.G.S.; an account of native Australian *Geraniaceae*, by Mr Robert Swinbourne of the Botanic Gardens, Adelaide; and a detailed paper on plant naming by the Nomenclature Committee of the New South Wales Geranium Society which, however, was not represented at the conference. The book contains 66 pages and can be obtained on application to The

All My Love (REGAL)

Australian Geranium Council at Box 915. H. G.P.O., Adelaide, South Australia.

The Council embraces the following societies:

The Canberra Geranium Society;

The Australian Geranium Society, Queensland Division;

The South Australian Geranium and Pelargonium Society;

The Australian Pelargonium and Geranium Society, Foundation Society, Victoria;

and

The West Australian Geranium Society.

The enthusiasm of the Australians is indicated by the vast distances they were prepared to travel in order to attend the conference.

The New South Wales division of the Australian Geranium

Princess of Wales (REGAL)

Society, a very lively group, became interested in taxonomy several years ago, when it began sorting out the names of cultivated varieties of pelargoniums. In 1969, it was invited by the Commission for Horticultural Science to assume the position of international registration authority for pelargoniums; it accepted in February, 1970. This entails a tremendous amount of research: all Australian cultivars will be dealt with first, it is hoped, whereafter the scope of the work will be extended world-wide—surely an infinite task, for which the society deserves all admiration.

The N.S.W. division seeks the co-operation of other societies in this project. Any communication should be addressed to Mrs Jean Llewellyn, Nyndee, Torokina Ave., St. Ives, 2075, N.S.W., Australia.

Ethel James, bred from Francis James

The Australian Pelargonium and Geranium Society, Foundation Society, Victoria, the first geranium society to be founded in Australia, was formed in 1956 by Mr John R. Blackman. It issues journals every December, March, June, and September and has many branches including one in Geelong, where the first pelargonium conservatory was built. Mr Blackman eventually moved to Alice Springs, taking his collection of plants with him. He has been instrumental in introducing new blood lines from the species, including *frutetorum*, into the cultivated varieties. One of the society's earliest and most energetic members was the late Mr W. H. Heytman, a tremendous correspondent and an early member of the B.P.G.S. He gave a great deal of encouragement to growers in all parts of the world and never failed to forward information on request.

The society's Hon. Secretary is Mr K. Byron, 11 Byron Street, Box Hill South, 3128, Victoria.

Canada

"Growing rooms", i.e., chambers with artificial lighting, have been used in England for many years by research establishments and universities, because they allow some control over a plant's environment. Much knowledge has been obtained on various aspects of growth, such as the effect of artificial lighting on the flowering period and the possibility of increasing it to a whole year.

For many years, I had been trying to find a responsible person in Canada willing to form a specialist society, but had met with little success until autumn 1971, when Mr Frank Goldring came to England to seek advice on growing-room culture of pelargoniums. My difficulty in getting a society off the ground in Canada was no doubt due to the shortness of summers in that country and the intense cold of the winters, making it impossible, or at any rate prohibitively expensive, to keep pelargoniums in glasshouses. Plants have had to be imported by the million from America every spring.

However, enormous enthusiasm is now raging in Canada for growing all kinds of plants in the basements of dwelling houses, a trend encouraged, no doubt, by the widespread use of central heating. From Mr Goldring's account of his growing rooms and the pictures of them that he has sent me, I can well understand why this method of cultivation is catching on; it is even easy to propagate cuttings under these conditions.

After a long talk in London and a personal visit to my home, Mr Goldring agreed to take a certain amount of literature back to Canada to help him form a specialist society there. Thanks to his great enthusiasm, such a society was formed on 12 January, 1972. He had the good fortune to get on the air, and also spoke to many influential horticultural people; it seems that the future of the society is now assured; the keenness

Hula

of the members radiates from their autumn 1972 journal which contains an account of their very successful first show.

Contact can be made with the society at 105 Dolly Varden Bvd., Scarborough 772, Ontario, Canada.

The International Association of Pelargonium Breeders

This venture has been started only recently. It is an informational body which, it is hoped, will be of immense value to breeders all over the world. It should be of interest to fanciers also, who will be able to read about new varieties as soon as they are introduced.

Mr Hamilton Tyler has agreed to be the Director. It was thought that the guiding hand should not be that of a breeder: Mr Tyler is a pelargonium historian, and writes on many other subjects as well, having several books to his credit. He is a most fortunate choice as Director and Recorder of the new association.

At intervals still to be decided on, all members will be sent newsletters containing information received such as personal experiences, chromosome counts, new varieties, individual goals, etc.

One very important purpose is to keep records of all the varieties originated by members: name, date, type or class, and a brief description. There will be no red tape and no evaluation by the association. A breeder about to introduce a new variety would record it; should the name be a duplication of one already used, the Recorder would immediately inform him of the fact. What a simple way of solving some of the problems of name duplication, at least within the membership.

All pelargonium breeders, professional or amateur, who are interested in joining the association or learning more about it are invited to write to: Mr Hamilton Tyler, 8450 West Dry Creek Road, Healdsburg, California 95448, U.S.A.

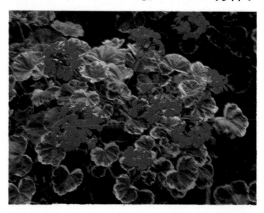

Improved Flower of Spring
(SILVER LEAF)

Mrs. Quilter (GOLDEN BRONZE)

Dark red Irene
(ZONAL)

Aztec (REGAL). Grown by D. A. Stilwell

Springtime

Strawberry Sundae. Grown by R. Wrelton

Santa Maria. Grown by R. Wrelton

Michael (REGAL). Grown by A. V. Mitchell

Plum Grand Slam. Grown by A. V. Mitchell

Orange Masterpiece

Fancy Free (FRUTETORUM)

Rhodamine (REGAL)

Index

DATE DUE			